About the Author

Born in Warsaw, Poland, she was ten years old when WWII started. Her parents perished in Treblinka, and she survived the war with her aunt under an assumed name. She came to England after the war as a refugee, with a group of surviving children from Europe, where she went to school and college.

Married early in life and enjoyed a career as dancer choreographer, and actress in six different countries including New York where she received an MA in Theatre Arts from Hunter College.

As well as *Bits And Pieces of My Life* Ruth has written a biography *My Son the Addict.*

She now lives with her husband in London and still pursues her acting career.

BITS AND PIECES OF MY LIFE

BY

RUTH POSNER

First printed 2002
Revised and reprinted 2012

Published by R & MSP Publishing

ISBN: 978-1-4717-7151-4

To my husband Michael

Forward

The following is an introduction to my book written nearly 10 years ago and revisited.

I have lately become obsessed by time, no wonder because I think I have so little left of it
Having reached fourscore years sharpens the brain and increases the awareness of the passage of time, the future shortens the past extends.

Great writers like Shakespeare could put it concisely in one sentence. Prospero says in the TEMPEST and I repeat this to myself many times

''Now my charms are all o'erthrown
And what strength I have
is my own which is most faint''

So to make most of the strength which is left however faint becomes an obsession
It is now 10 years since I wrote my story I shelved it for many reasons and wish to revive it now before a real lethargy sets in and before time ceases to exist.
It is in this frame of mind that the following poem crept into my head

Outrunning Time

I am always rushing!
I notice I don't walk.
I run from one room to another
I don't know why I am always in a hurry -
it's as though I am running out of time,

Time is chasing me,
How much time do I have left?
I am running out of time, yes…
I am running out of life.

I have no time to do the things I want to
Because I need time to do them now….
Even though there's nothing
I have to do today.
(It's not today I need the time for-
It's maybe for next week, next month
And that is the problem.)

I might not have the time to do things then
Because I might not be here.
So even though today is free

I am rushing and chasing in a hurry
To catch up with life.

There is so little time:
Make each moment precious,
Savour it while you can
(That's a lot of bollocks)

Give me time instead,
(and I will outrun it, I swear).

Ruth Posner   2012

My thanks to
Angela Meredith for editing my "Time" poem and
Patrick Rylands for his photography and design advice

Introduction

This is a story of recollections and reflections of my experience written over a long period as the mood caught me - with many stops and starts. Some have told it better, many have suffered more. Since the events of the 2nd World War we know there were many other tragedies and other holocausts, despite our enormous technological advancement humanity has not changed that much.

This however is my story and I dedicate it to the memory of my son.

I also wish to thank my husband, Michael, whose encouragement and assistance made this possible.

June 2002

New York - 1980

I thought this is the time to start. I began to have conversations with myself, I don't mean walking through the streets of New York waving my arms about, gesticulating wildly, a sight not uncommon in this crazy Metropolis, I just mean reflecting as I walk along on my way to the supermarket or some studio for a class about my life, about my reasons for being here.

My decision to tell you my story came to me really at that point when I realised how many things have happened to me during the course of my life, how varied my life has been, like a book with many unfinished chapters, a bit disjointed. I need some kind of a link, a thread to put the pieces in order before it all evaporates and the memory fades away.

I must get hold of it all now and this is the only way I know how.

I am not going to embroider or embellish to keep you interested but rather to tell you as it was.

August 1980 or thereabouts, I am never quite sure of precise dates. Whether things happened on Friday or Saturday has never been important to me the main thing is they happened. Anyway, August 1980 I am holding a rolled up piece of paper which I received from Hunter College, New York. It is my Master of Arts degree for which I have worked the last 3 years.

I am quite proud of it since at my age, I am 45 and with very little prior education, I consider it quite an achievement. I normally have very little faith in my academic ability and my conventional education amounts to nil although I have always had intellectual aspirations.

I have to confess something to you which really bugs me I cannot do even simple arithmetic because my educational biological clock stopped at the age of 10 when the war broke out and I never caught up. Like bicycle riding or swimming, skills not acquired at a certain age seem so much more difficult to master at a later age; though I admit this might be an excuse for my numerical dislexsia. My poor father tried very hard to teach me some mathematics which must have been a very frustrating experience. So let me cast my mind back to my "crazy" childhood

Poland -1939

I vaguely remember German tanks rolling through the streets of our town. I was looking out of the window of our street-level flat, a strange feeling of excitement came over me, it spelled danger. How little I knew the extent of it. It was to interrupt the routine of every day life. I was frightened and fascinated by the strangers in uniforms with their helmets and swastikas bearing an air of power and victory.

I remember my father's sad face as he held my hand and said that whatever happens we should stay together. My mother, the eternal optimist, said something about the Poles will never let themselves be occupied for long and it will all be over soon. Our hopes and illusions were soon to be shattered. No one envisaged what was to come. The Germans, as we now know, devised a clever system. There was not too much panic at the very beginning.

Stage one was the confiscation of some household goods especially radios and the evacuation of Polish Jews from the centre of the town to other prescribed areas of the city. It was not called Ghetto yet.

We moved out of our flat and went to live with my aunt, her husband and their two small children then aged 5 and 7. It was then that I became ill and in retrospect it was fortunate that it was then and not later. My illness started as simple appendix, which was operated on by my cousin who was a surgeon, but complications developed because of the primitive operating conditions and the lack of anti-biotics. I developed gangrene and according to what was told to me much later, I was close to death, because of perforated peritoneum. The wound did not heal properly for a long time; I was lucky to be alive.

Stage two, I was still convalescing and one day I looked out of the window and saw two SS men beating an old Jew and viciously pulling at his long beard. Shocked and bewildered I run to my mother who could offer no explanation for this beastly behaviour which became a not uncommon occurrence in days to come. We were now issued the yellow star armbands and it was compulsory to wear them. My mother came home one day and told us that she was stopped by a uniformed Nazi soldier who asked her what she was doing wearing a yellow star. My mother looked 100%. Aryan, she was a tall woman with high cheekbones, straight nose and blue-gray eyes and she obviously did not fit the German idea of a stereotypical Jewess. She however did assure him that she was one! It was soon after this incident that SS men came to our door and gave us an hour to get out of our flat and only take some personal belongings. We were being evacuated into a Ghetto and our families had to split up. I remember my mother saying to one of the officers, "You wear a black shirt but your heart can't be black too". His answer was to punch her in the face and I shall never forget the look on her face, shock and shame that I should witness such gross and ungentlenmanly behaviour.

My mother, father and I moved into the Ghetto where we were assigned to one room which was in a corner of a house; we were separated from my aunt and her children, here other families were already occupying the rest of the rooms. We had to share a rather large and dirty kitchen. There wasn't much food and my parents dispaired; they also wanted to know what happened to the rest of our family.

This strange force of circumstance put us in touch with Jews with whom we normally had not come in contact. Most of them spoke Yiddish which I did not understand. We were, so called, assimilated Jews. We had many Christian friends as well as assimilated Jews like us with whom we had a lot more in common than the strangers with whom we now were sharing our destiny.

One day I had a visitor. A Christian school-girl friend of mine came to see me. I can't remember how she managed to find me although it was possible, of course, for Christian Poles to move freely whilst we were no longer allowed beyond the enclosure of the Ghetto. I remember very clearly my sense of shame. I did not want her to see me in this place.

Deep down I felt that maybe I had done something terrible of which I was not aware and this is why I was here. She sensed my discomfort and after a short and awkward conversation which did not reveal our feelings, we said goodbye. The first of many goodbyes to people I was never to see again.

One night we were awakened by loud banging on the doors and German voices shouting,"Juden Heraus," (Jews Out). Panic stricken we looked out of the window to see some of our neighbours being pushed into the courtyard. My father told us to quickly get on the floor under the beds. We did so; we were afraid to breathe. The Germans were inside the house rounding up people. We heard shots being fired and the sound of trucks driving off. Deportation to the camps had began and still we were not fully aware of the full extent of the horror. The SS soldiers did not open our door, since our room was tucked away in the corner of a long corridor or maybe they had a full quota. I shall never know. The fact that we survived round one did not make us feel better; my father began to fear worse things to come. He conceived a plan of which I was not aware at the time. His main purpose was to save me. It was only much later I was told by my aunt that he was loosing faith in the possibility of his own survival. Much what followed happened more by chance than by design. My father met, in the Ghetto, a friend who prior to the war was a factory owner manufacturing leather goods. He was now employed by the Germans making rucksacks for the German army and was allowed to employ, with permission, a few Jews and at that time was allowed only two further permits. He agreed to take two of us. It was then that my father decided to send me away together with my aunt, Lola, my mother's sister.

It is only after many years of going over the same well trodden past that I think I understood my father's decision. My mother needed his protection and she would never agree to go with me to the factory and leave my father behind.

My mother was the essence of warmth and kindness which was often attributed to naivete or weakness. I remember stories father told me about her. Before the war when buying strawberries from a peasant woman she would inquire how long it would take her to fill a basket and since it was such a back-breaking job why didn't she charge more money. On another occasion she took off her dress and gave it to a woman whose plight she considered much worse than hers. My aunt, Lola, on the other hand was a tougher woman. She managed to find a temporary 'safe haven' for her own children with a Polish peasant hidden in the country while her own husband was 'safe' for the time being working for the Jewish Juden's Raat (a small number of Jews employed by the Germans as organisers in the Ghetto) My father obtained the two permits for me and my aunt to work in the factory and two years were added to my age to make me more elligible for work.

With our work permits and a small grain of hope I had to say good-bye to my parents whose faces will stay imprinted on my mind forever. My mother was speechless and my father not wanting to betray his anxiety assured me that this was the only way.

My aunt and I were put on a truck which took us to the Kromolowsky leather factory outside Warsaw. Here we were immediately put to work. We were assigned our stools and shown how to operate the machines. I was too young and too clumsy and I immediataly got into trouble for not doing the job diligently. Our overseers were women who were party members and some were so-called Folks-Deutsch people, Poles working for the Germans.

On one occasion I was pushed off the stool by one of these women and severely reprimanded for dropping a stitch and generally not coping with the workload. My aunt came to my defense and tried to explain that the muddle I was getting into was due to my appendix operation from which I still had not fully recovered. The overseers response was a strong kick in my stomach. I learned a bitter lesson there and then. I have never been fully committed since then to the idea that women because of their maternal instinct are devoid of cruelty.

Only years later I learned that my aunt bribed our, so called, foreman by giving him some jewelry which she had sewn into her corset. For a short while I was left alone.

It was here, strangely enough, that I had my first sexual encounter. I remember a young boy 15 or 16 years old who was also one of the 'inmates'. He used to take me down to the boiler room and there we would talk, cuddle and kiss and dream.

One shining star in bleak horizon. This too was soon to be denied because what followed brought us face to face with the uncertainty of our situation.

The living conditions in the factory were less than primitive. We slept on thin mats in a big attic space; women on one side, men on the other. There was one cold water tap for up to 50 people. Once a week we were marched to the local public baths near the city; maybe the hygiene conscious Germans were afraid of the possible spread of disease. It was on one of the marches to the baths that we were stopped in the middle of the road and the segregations had began. We had no idea what was happening. Women were ordered to one side, men the other; friends and families were divided and people began to scream and shout, panic and chaos broke out. Shots were heard and all I remember was clinging, terrified to my aunt when all of a sudden a man standing by a German soldier on the pavement pulled us out on to the pavement saying something to the German to whom the German officer nodded. The man was a friend of our family who as I mentioned before was one of those Jews selected by the Germans to help in the 'organisation'. The Germans were very clever in their deceptions always preventing the possible irruption of chaos and disorder. These 'helpers' were not traitors since they had no idea as to the overall plans. They were selected by the Germans to do their bidding, in doing so they thought they were helping their fellow Jews. Very often they too were disposed of subsequently.

This friend pulled us out to prevent us from being send to a harder labour camp where the 'selected' people were being sent. He told us that in the Ghetto which we had left hundreds of Jews with academic degrees have been saved and evacuated to Palestine. He said that it was possible that my parents might have gone as well. My aunt told me that this was impossible since my parents would never agree to such move without me and that they to some means of communication, the nature of which she did not disclose.

We were told to go back to the factory and it was only much much later that we have learned of the plight of those who were supposedly sent to Palestine. They were in fact taken to a cemetery outside the town where they were machine gunned. Thus were some of the intelligencia disposed of.

We went back to work in the factory. My aunt on one occasion took the opportunity to tell me that she had an agreement with my mother in the event of anything happening to her, my mother would try and leave a dress in which she had sewn some family jewels.

Life in the factory took it's toll, we were permanently hungry but such is the human spirit that we would sometimes get together and talk about favourite dishes, inventing meals and imagining submerging our tired bodies in hot baths and luxuriating. We slept on the floors on very thin mats covered with threadbare blankets.

I remember one very humiliating experience. I had just washed my thick hair in the only cold water tub available and managed to twist it into two heavy ringlets. Even under these conditions a young girl's vanity seemed to triumph as I wanted to impress my boyfriend, however I noticed him staring at my forehead with great intensity. He finally told me that there were two lice creeping down my forehead! Ashamed and shocked I run away crying and threw myself on my mat feeling hopeless, dirty and abandoned. That image has stayed with me since then.

Far worse was yet to come. We were told one day that there was an evacuation from the Ghetto and that nearly all the inhabitants were deported. A friend of my mother's brought us one of my mother's dresses.

On seeing this my aunt became deathly pale. I shall never know how the friend got hold of the dress and it was only later that I learned about that pact my mother made with my aunt regarding the dress and it's contents..

The realisation that I shall never see my parents again filled me with unimaginable horror and desolation. I   could not be comforted or helped in my grief made worse when, a few days later, my aunt heard that her two children, aged 5 and 7, who were hiding with a Polish peasant woman were denounced either by the peasant or a neighbour. No one really knew exactly what happened to them. They were either shot on the spot or taken into a camp where they perished. They vanished never to be heard of again.

As I am writing this I am conscious of how easily the letters are formed, how easily the hand moves forming those words and how hard it is to believe that it all actually happened.

I don't know to this day what gave my aunt the strength to go on and plan an escape for us. She told me years later that it was a conscious decision. She contemplated taking her own life but having looked at me, and realising my vulnerabilty she knew she had to go on. I only realized the pain she must have suffered when I had my own son. I cannot put it into words and I trust that you know what I mean. There are no words to describe such emotions. The depth of such emotions render us speechless or makes us howl like animals. What gives us the strength to go on I shall never know.

My aunt devised a plan for our escape. Time was running out.

Today, 1995, is the 50th anniversary of the Holocaust. There is a great deal of coverage in the media. There are two strongly felt emotions - why do we need to bring it all up again, there are so many disasters happening all over the world, Bosnia, Ruanda, Tibet to mention but a few? Why is it that the Jews think they are the only people who have a monopoly on suffering? I can't answer these nor am I going to pontificate on which is the greater suffering. All I know is that I am in my 60's now, the past and the present are closing and I want the memory of my parents immortalised. The thought that when I die their lives will be forgotten is abhorrent to me. Even the photographs will fade and vanish. Had they died a natural deaths the finality of their lives would be quite acceptable but they were brutally murdered for no other reason than they were Jewish and it happened in a civilised country; a country which produced Goethe and Beethoven and many other great artists.

Why is there so much hatred in this world? I know that we cannot extend love to wherever it is needed; only saints can do that but why do we spend so much energy on hating?

I was instructed in the escape plan and given an address to hide in my shoe so that if anything happened to my aunt I could appeal to that person whose name I now held under my foot. The plan was very simple or so it seemed. We were marched once a week to a public bath in the town; the Germans were after all very hygiene conscious nation. We marched in the middle of the road with SS soldiers on either side of us with guns and bayonets ready for action. The idea behind the plan was that as my aunt and I went to the shower we would first go to the toilet and I would pretend to be sick. We would wait there as long as possible and when the coast was clear we would run out and run across the street to the Aryan side of the town. It was winter time and already dark during the shower period. The risk was tremendous since had we been noticed running we would have been shot on the spot. We also knew that the possibility of survival was better than the certainty of death had we stayed. The arrangement was that if we crossed the road successfully my aunt was to get in touch with someone who had a car waiting for us with false passports and documents.

I do not know the precise details of how she managed to mastermind the escape and arrange the details. It was dark and I do remember being in the lavatory and shaking with fear and on a agreed signal coming out of the lavatory, holding my aunt's hand and casually walking out to the other side of the road - the side of LIFE. We were so lucky it was dark and no one saw us. It was such a blatant act, maybe the Germans were not capable of suspecting anyone for performing this under the circumstances.

In later years when I became an Actress my aunt would say that this was my greatest performance.

We did not dare to be too optimistic since we had a long journey in front of us, there were many checkpoints on the road and we had so little time to assume our new personnae. It all seemed like a dream. We went to the spot where the car was supposed to be waiting. We did not have to wait long, a car drew up, we got in and no one spoke a word. It was like a scene from a silent film. As the car sped along my aunt began to drill me in my new life story. I was ill and needed country air and my aunt was the fiance of my father who was in the Polish army, my own mother having died at birth, so my future stepmother was now looking after me.

On the way to a country village we were stopped, as we knew we might be, at a German checkpoint. As they checked our papers my aunt whispered to me to smile. Which I did, with a hand on my heart which was beating loudly and so fast I was convinced that everyone would hear.

We arrived at a little country cottage and my aunt relayed our story to the owner, a peasant farmer, who accepted it without question and showed us to our little room with welcoming high beds.

Here the 'performance' continued. Despite being exhilarated by our luck so far and extremely tired, my aunt wanting to prove what good catholics we were made me kneel beside my bed, leaving the door ajar so that our landlord could see me make the sign of a cross and hear me recite the Lord's prayer. Ironically I knew the prayer better than any Jewish religious prayer.

I remember how happy I was to be still alive and how guilty I felt about those who remained behind. My aunt had to look after me now knowing that her own two children and her husband were killed. My feelings for her were very confused I wanted to please her to prove myself worthy of her attention but at the same time I resented her for not being my mother and for suspecting that even in her subconscious mind she harboured a deep resentment that I was alive and her own children were so brutally murdered.

These feelings still remain with me 50 years later.......

Every day in which we were still alive was a bonus. We never felt safe knowing that one wrong word one wrong look could betray us.

Such fate has already befallen other members of our family. My aunt's brother and sister were also hiding under assumed names They were in the town of Lvov on the Aryan side of the town. They were both recognised by a Folks-Deutsch Pole working for the Germans. They were spared the horrors of concentration camps since they were arrested and shot on the spot.

I realise now as I am writing this that it all sounds so improbable that maybe I should fill in more details but I will not embroider the facts. I only know that it happened.

We could stay in the cottage only for a limited time and it was now time to go back to Warsaw. My aunt found some accommodation in a flat through an advertisement in a local paper. We were living off the jewelry sown in my mother's dress which my aunt sold or used as bribes.

I should point out here that our luck in surviving thus far was partly due to the fact that neither of us looked particularly Jewish and we spoke a pure unaccented Polish since we never knew or spoke Yiddish. The only Jewish characteristic in my appearance was my dark and curly hair which I often covered with a kerchief or pulled tightly behind my ears.

The people, in whose flat we now had a room, owned a china shop. The story was that we were selling our few belongings since our house was bombed by the Germans and my father was lost at the front and so we needed to work. It was agreed that I could help a little in the shop and my aunt could help the busy lady in some house work.

I remember one incident which paralysed me with fear. I was alone with the owner of the shop who seemed very friendly. He offered me a cup of coffee and asked me to be so kind and climb up a ladder to re-arrange some mugs on the upper shelves. As I was doing this I felt his hand creeping up under my skirt. Not fully realising what was going on I looked down and noticed a strange look in his eyes, he said " you sure that you are not a little Zyduwechka?, which means little Jewess, an 'endearing' insult often used by Poles. I do not know what gave me the strength not to fall of the ladder because my legs shook so much but I remember saying 'what a crazy idea' this was and that I would tell my aunt and his wife how he insulted me for thinking that. I nothing of the incident to my aunt; the shame was even greater than the fear.

It is strange how one can press the fast reverse button in one's brain and the images come flooding in and every detail stands out magnified.

I learned one positive thing from all my experiences. Whenever I feel depressed I think of the many lucky escapes and of the fact that my parents died such untimely death when they were only half my present age and that every day of my life is a bonus. These are sobering thoughts.

1942 Warsaw Uprising

The Jewish Ghetto, now demolished, is full of ghosts and memories of those we remember and those we never knew. I will not try to tell you the details of the suffering and of the inhumanities perpetrated there. This has been all documented in books, films and personal stories.

I remember standing with my aunt at a window looking out not saying a word, but both of us thinking the same thoughts, there behind those walls so many lives were lost and we are here, 'the other side,' and feeling so lucky to be alive but also feeling guilty. I think that consciously or unconsciously that sense of guilt gave us courage to play our part in the Warsaw Uprising on the Aryan side. It gave us the possibility of fighting the enemy.

The uprising was doomed from the start. The Russians were supposed to come to the rescue but nothing of that sort happened. Many Poles fought valiantly and many lost their lives. I remember throwing bottles of petrol at German tanks risking the possibility of being shot at and feeling quite heroic running for cover with bullets whizzing over my head. There were tremendous food shortages. We were sharing a house with a number of Polish underground fighters all sharing in meagre food rations, mainly potatoes. We felt a tremendous bondage, united against common enemy. I don't know how the Polish underground fighters would have felt about us had they known that we were Jewish. I would like to think that there were some good people amongst them to whom it would have made no difference but we never put it to test.

The fighting lasted for about two weeks after which the Poles capitulated and the Germans victorious again began to evacuate the whole of Warsaw leaving only the very old and the very young. And so we became prisoners-of-war and a new chapter in my life began.

We were rounded up and told that anyone declared a prisoner-of-war who dared to stay behind would be executed. We were marched to trains and taken to Germany thinking that whatever fate awaited us could not be as horrendous as the fate our families suffered.

My life as a prisoner-of-war was hard and not exactly an ideal way of spending one's adolescence but it was by all accounts a paradise compared to Auschwitz or Treblinka. My aunt worked in the kitchen and was able to either get or steal an extra ration of bread and potatoes. I cleaned the snow off the local railway lines and listened to the stories of other prisoners reflecting on love, life, politics etc. This was my school and my playground and it is amazing how normal it all felt after the passage of time. One day, an Italian prisoner from a nearby camp who fell in love with one of the Polish young women, brought some good news. The war was coming to an end, the allies were approaching and the Germans were becoming scared. The cold, discomfort and constant nagging hunger were fading into insignificance and we were overjoyed on hearing the good news. One day however, we were told that we were being transferred to another prison- of-war camp. The girl friend of the Italian prisoner cried bitterly knowing, I suppose, that she will never see him again. We collected our meagre belongings and we were put on a train destination unknown.

Years later in talking about the event with my aunt, she told me what was really at stake. The Germans apparently decided that all enemies be it Jews or Poles or Gypsies should be disposed of as quickly as possible.

The war was coming to an end and all the German enemies were to perish. We were bundled into trains to meet the same fate of those no longer with us although we did not know it at the time. The train in which we were travelling passed through Essen, a large industrial city. The train suddenly stopped, there was a shrieking noise from the sky as American bombers began an air raid on what they must have perceived to be a military target. The train doors opened and the German guards as well as its strange passengers, including my aunt and I, scrambled for cover. The planes descended lower and began spraying us with machine-gun fire. We were now the enemies of those above us; how could they have known that we were not Germans? A heavy weight pushed me to the ground and I lay still under it not daring to breathe. When the planes left I heard my aunt calling my name. I cried out, not being able to move, terrified that my aunt will not be able to find me, when I felt the weight being lifted off my body. It was the body of a dead woman killed by the machine-gun fire. Someone died in order to save me. I felt a hand grabbing me and someone calling, "lets run before the Germans pull themselves together". Fortunately it was dark and we ran to a nearby wooded area where we hid among the trees. One more escape from the jaws of death.

We spent the whole night in the woods and at dawn we walked till we came to a small farm. I can not remember how many of us there were but my aunt who spoke very good German, appealed to the farmer explaining we were indeed prisoners-of-war, were harmless, hungry and willing to do any work in exchange for some food and shelter.

There is a sequel to this above story which I shall tell you about now in case it slips my memory. Years and years later after I got married and we lived in

London we met an American couple with whom we became friendly. Corrine was a journalist and Frank used to have his own commercial film advertising company. One day I was telling Frank about a radio play in which I had the role of a German mother superior, not exactly type casting! The play was about a team of bomber pilots in the RAF who had flown 35 missions and how the team slowly disintegrated when some of them did not return from their missions. Courage and dedication to the cause was not enough when faced with the possible loss of life. I asked Frank what kind of mettle is a man made of who sits in the cockpit of a plane dropping tools of utter destruction while at the same time doubting the possibility of survival. Frank listened carefully to what I was saying and then replied "I know exactly what you are talking about because I was there".

"But what did you do ? " I asked, "I was a bomber pilot during the war and I flew 35 missions. One of the worst experiences was flying over Essen when we had to spray the station with machine-gun fire and seeing the poor German bastards running in a panic". Frank could not believe it when I told him that, probably, I was one of the poor "bastards" and that in a strange way he may have actually contributed to saving me since if it weren't for the bombing a much worse fate had waited us. So now I can get back to my story.

When, after hiding in the woods, we came to the German village and asked the first farmer we saw for water to our great amazement that German farmer took us in. They, of course, did not know that there were Jews among us. I peeled mountains of potatoes and learned how to milk cows and my aunt helped with cleaning and cooking; the two young men who were also with us became farmhands. To have solid food every day, albeit stodgy, was a luxury. We stayed on that farm until the end of the war was declared and there I learned whatever German I know.

Allied soldiers appeared in the village bearing chocolates and cigarettes, distributing them freely to the local farmers.

I remember one strange incident. On discovering that we were Poles one of the American officers asked us if we knew of any German soldiers who might be hiding in the village. There were in fact two Wermacht, ordinary German soldiers, hiding in the attic of the farm house. My aunt knew about it. The farmer's wife stood there when the American officer asked the question, her wide open eyes spoke volumes. The two soldiers in the attic were in fact her nephews. My aunt replied promptly and with great conviction that to her knowledge there was no one hiding. Had they been members of the Gestapo I feel certain that she would not have been so generous but they were, after all, ordinary soldiers caught in the war machine and whose family took us in when we were desperate and in need of help.

After the departure of the American officers, my aunt and the farmer's wife embraced without words. An eloquent moment which spelt some hope for the human race.

The time had come now for us to say goodbye and to move on. We were free with uncertain future but we were free! Our plight and status had now improved enormously; we were taken this time by the English contingent to a RAF station in Detmold, a town not far from the village where we had been living. It was quite hard to say goodbye to our "saviours".

My aunt told me years later that the farmer's wife was really sorry to see us go because her son had grown to like me and was ready to wait for me to grow up and be his wife.

For us a new chapter had began.

In Detmold we were offered a room and asked to help in the officer's mess. My task was to set the tables for breakfast and my aunt again was helping in the kitchen as well as translating whenever necessary.

In a lighter vain I have to mention that with all her culinary experience during the war years she never learned to cook and is the world's worst cook.

I was now trying to accustom my ears to the English language. I remember that the first English word I heard was "Curly" which became my nickname. My hair was dark, thick and curly and much admired; the very hair I was trying to hide under scarves fearing it would betray my Jewish identity.

Setting tables for breakfast I discovered the delights of peanut butter and marmalade not then known on the Continent even in prewar days. Each morning I devoured teaspoonfuls of both. It was sheer heaven. I have to remind you that our true identity was still hidden and my assumed name was Irena Slabovska.

One day my aunt called me to say that she had something of great importance to tell to me. A young girl, who was sharing a room with us, was serving supper in the Officer's Mess and as she put a plate of ham and salad in front of one of the RAF officers he said in very good German that he did not eat ham, would she return it to the kitchen and tell the cook the meal was for Squadron Leader Scott; he would understand. The girl was visibly shaken and broke into tears. He asked her why and she explained that she too was Jewish, realised he was and begged him not to tell the persons, my aunt and me, she was sharing the room with as they were Poles and might harm her. He demanded to see my aunt who burst into tears of great relief and joy as she revealed the true nature of our identity.

Yet another new chapter of my life began

Sydney Scott had many conversations with my aunt. He was committed to helping in any way he could. They decided that it would be best for me to come to England and resume my much neglected education.

England had a quota of refugee children under 15 and I was young enough to qualify. My aunt's husband had relatives in Brussels who might have survived the war. Although not permitted officially Sydney somehow found a way to smuggle her into Belgium.

My own feelings I remember were very mixed, a sense of rejection, a tinge of fear but above all a feeling of excitement for the new future facing me and a new life about to begin.

Sydney Scott made all the necessary arrangements and I found myself saying goodby to my aunt. We had gone through so much together and from now we were to carve out seperate paths. I was on my own though not alone. I arrived in England with a refugee children transport.

There were 50 of us, mainly Polish, Austrian and Hungarian Jewish children. Our first port of call was Southampton. I remember a big house called Wintershill Hall. Long corridors, a huge dining room where we all took our meals and big bedrooms, one of which I shared with five others. One of the girls was Hungarian with a lovely kind smile and sad intelligent eyes; her name was Edith. We soon became friends even though we had no common language; we communicated in rather bad German. Edith was the first person to whom I confided my big secret. Even though both of us went through so much in our young lives we had our dreams and we had our fantasies. I told Edith that what I really wanted to be was an actress however I felt ashamed because it seemed so frivolous and also I had no idea how to go about it. Edith on the other hand wanted to go to college and become a Montessori kindergarten teacher. She never told me much about her family except that her parents were killed and that she had four surviving sisters out of a family of seven. She was very proud of two of her sisters who were good painters; they were some years older than Edith and were attempting to get to Israel.

The highlight of my stay in Wintershill Hall was one day when a BBC radio team came to visit in order to interview us and I was asked to sing a Polish folksong. My desire to seize any opportunity to perform was unquenchable.

Our first English lessons were given by a German professor, Dr.Schneider, who was himself a refugee and came to England just before the war. I remember the day Dr. Schneider asked us what we wanted to do with our lives. Most of the slightly older children expressed a wish to learn various trades in order to become independent as soon as possible. The rest of us who were a bit younger wanted to go to school in order to make up for the lost time. Witek, one of the boys, wanted to become a doctor and I learned years later that he succeeded. Edith and I were the only girls who desperately wanted to go back to school. Edith who by now was like my sister, expressed her desire to stay with me if we could manage to go to school. I cannot remember exactly how long we were at Wintershill Hall.

We were introduced to two German Jewish women, Sophie and Hilda, who ran a hostel for refugee children in Reading. They were good friends of Doctor Schneider and on his recommendation they agreed to accept Edith and me in the hostel and to enable us to continue our education there. They knew of a good school in Reading and also knew the headmistress who they were sure would be glad to give us a place. Thus we were enrolled in Kendrick High School for Girls.

Years later, Sophie presented me with a little book in which I had written and described the experience of my first day in an English school. I was 16 years old at the time, my English was limited but my thoughts and feelings were clear, so I shall just quote to you what I had written in my little book.

'The first thought that came to me was, after so many years I shall return to school, I will sit at my desk, I shall possess school books again. A teacher will talk to me in a foreign language. I will meet a number of happy girls, school girls who will go to their homes every day and who will tell their mothers about the two foreign girls who came to their class and they couldn't even speak English. So here we were my friend Edith and I sitting in front of 20 curious faces staring at us. The teacher kindly said a few words of introduction. It was a geography lesson and the teacher asked the girls to take out their atlases and find the countries both of us came from.' Poland and Hungary' repeated the girls with a strange tune in their voices. "Oh! it is not in England" noticed one of them, a great disappointment reflected in her round face. Their eyes were running restlessly through our bodies starting from the bottom of our shoes, and examining carefully every detail of our appearance. Perhaps they have never seen any foreign people before and maybe they were really disappointed that we looked like any ordinary human being. The lesson seemed to us eternal. I hated them and I envied them they could make any remark they liked. After the lesson was finished they all began gathering around us. "Oh! please say something in Polish, say something in Hungarian" It was such fun for them, but I wanted to get away and not being able to say very much and fearing that my face will betray my thoughts I went

out of the class pulling my friend behind me. On my way to the hostel I thought ' most exhausting day has passed and many other days will follow this one I will.....perhaps.....manage!

Thus began a new phase in my life.

Sophie and Hilde were serious pedagogues and ran the hostel with typical German efficiency and thriftiness. Life was austere and puritanical.

I found it difficult because despite the wounds I carried inside me, my zest for life was unquenchable. I felt a heavy weight was placed on my shoulders and my adolescence was quickly turning to old age. The philosophy of Rudolph Steiner was the guiding principle in the hostel and vegetarianism strictly observed. Dates with boys were discouraged. I felt unsure of myself and inferior, academic achievement was much praised but with my sadly lacking tools of basic education I found some subjects like maths and science extremely difficult. My friend Edith was the teacher's pet. Very studious by nature she would sit for hours and do algebra for fun!

I so longed for love and acceptance but neither woodwork nor gardening, which was much encouraged, ignited my interest. I began to learn to play the flute and the piano which I loved but my fear of failure was greater than the joy of playing and I soon gave it up especially when I learned that the hostel had little money for such luxuries.

It was only years later I realised that they did what they could under difficult financial circumstances but that did not bring me back my youth and the craving for love and adventure. Also I realise now that it was the only environment which was conducive to study and in which I managed to learn English well enough to pass my School Certificate in 6 subjects. I still cherished my desire to go to a drama school but never expressed it for fear of appearing superficial.

Meeting Hilde and Sophie 40 years later I saw them in a different light and was very touched when they came to see a play I was in and expressed such pride and joy in seeing me in it. Now I see them as two quite extraordinary old ladies.

I was torn between two seperate worlds one the puritanical world of the hostel where values were always examined and many teenage fantasies, like dressing up, like dating, like wearing lipstick were definitely discouraged. My other world was lived during the school holidays with the Scotts in their house in Wembley.

Susie, Sydney's wife was an elegant Russian woman, vain with pretensions to cultural life of which she was really quite ignorant. Her feelings towards me were ambivelant. She gave me all sorts of pretty hand-me-down clothes which I felt guilty about wanting because I too wanted to look elegant. Susie was not a happy woman. Their marriage was an empty one since they did not share many interests in common.

Sydney and Susie wanted to adopt me but I did not want to change my name nor did I ever feel quite at home with them though I was very grateful to them for giving me a home during my school holidays.

One night when Susie was away from the house Sydney came to my room and lay beside me on my bed. I did not move and neither did he. He said he was cold and lonely and that it was a fatherly gesture. I did not know then how to respond. Although the incident was soon forgotten something in me died that day and I was no longer either grateful to him or affectionate.

I finished school and received my School Certificate. I really wanted to matriculate with the option of going to university but my lack of attainment in subjects like maths and sciences plus my natural lack of aptitude for such subjects made matriculation impossible. Some have regarded even my obtaining the school certificate in a new language as an achievement.

I stopped writing at this point............

Many months later I resume my story. I have stopped a number of times realising that my story is not all that unique. It is the story of many thousands of others who were lucky enough to survive; some of whom managed to write and record their experiences so much better.

I lost courage and the desire to regurgitate however it is now March 1993 and I am off again! I am now 63 years old and it all happened such a long time ago; I need a jolt, a stimulus to get me going again. Tonight, just by chance, I got that jolt. I watched a TV. programme made by Howard Jacobson, an English Jew, who set out on a personal quest to recapture his roots. The journey took him to Poland and Lithuania from where his grandparents came. He interviewed an older woman, one of the few remaining survivors from Wilno, he asked her why she stayed in the country so famous for Jew-hatred where even now 55 years after the Holocaust, Jewish graves have been desecrated.

What kind of hate is it that can kill twice, killing the ghosts of the dead, long buried?. This woman's reply hit me right below the belt. "Yes" she said " rising nationalism rekindled the cancerous malignancy of racial hatred but leaving the country would have meant letting Hitler achieve his goals of making the country Juden-frei , free of Jews.

So it is at this point that I cast my mind back again to pick up my story.

After obtaining my school certificate I compromised on my desire to become an actress and with the help of the Jewish Commitee for Refugees, which had supported me since my arrival in England I embarked on a career of a dance teacher and was accepted at the rather exclusive London College of Dance where I spend the next 3 years of my life. I was the only foreigner and the only Jew in an otherwise blue-blooded English environment. I was an object of some curiosity and even, at times, treated like a favourite pet. I learned a lot about the English class system. My command of English improved, though I spoke with an accent I had an upper-class tone which I picked up from those around me. This I later realised was useful in a class ridden society because I could not be 'placed'. The little foreigner could be the great grand daughter of the Russian Tsar. If this is what they wanted to believe. In my desire to be accepted I played the role to the full!

Now looking back at this experience I realise how much of the real me was lost in this process. I wanted to please, I wanted to be loved so I became everything to every one, playing many different parts. Maybe and this is only a conjecture, my secret desire to be an actress stems from the wish to be many characters. Anyway how can someone with a Polish accent be accepted in an English drama school; who would pay for me to indulge such desires?

The college offered a teacher's diploma which meant that I could get a job in a school. Being able to support myself was of primary importance although teaching clumsy school children to dance and organising end of term dance concerts was not my idea of heaven.

I was saved from this plight by meeting my future husband at one of the college‚Äôs end-of-term dances. I was usually pretty hopeless on these occasions. The young men invited to these dances were the chinless wonders from the Sandhurst Military Academy, terribly well spoken and not interested in anything serious apart from having jolly good time. I had nothing in common with them; though they found me reasonably attractive thought me rather strange. When talking to any of these young men about 'the meaning of life' I would see his eyes glaze over, eagerly looking for retreat.

I was a member of the party organising committee which was responsible for providing male partners. Since I had no such 'contacts' I asked a friend to bring as many male friends as she could muster. So, Michael, my future husband, turned up at a summer tea dance as a friend of a friend. Michael was a shy and sensitive young man, very different from all the others I have met so far. He talked about T.S. Elliot's poetry and the novels of Jean Paul Sartre. I was so impressed that he actually liked me since I did not consider myself worthy of his attention and though I liked him immensely I tried very hard to introduce him to other girls; maybe as a kind of test to see whether he would still like me above everyone else. I only by chance discovered that he was also Jewish.

My childhood experiences set me apart from my peers. I was always conscious of playing a role and of hiding the real me which was locked- up deep down and which I knew would never be understood. I now realised that the confused emotions I had were tearing me apart.

On one hand I needed someone so desperately, not just to be loved, a wish common to all men and women, but to be able to unburden myself, to open up, to tell how desperate I felt inside, how I missed my parents, how I wanted a family to belong to and above all to wash away the unbearable guilt I sometimes felt for being alive and being happy for being alive. I was also conscious of shame, as though it was my fault for not having parents, for being an orphan refugee helped by the Jewish Committee which not only paid for my education but also gave me money for a brief holiday in Ireland where

Michael's family were living, where we went so that I could meet his parents.

Michael and his family are very English and the English maybe because they protect their own feelings and are afraid of hurting others don't ask questions which might bring unhappy memories and in turn embarrass them. No one, including Michael, in the early years, has ever asked me anything about my childhood and my family. I think I understood this and accepted the situation in an existential way. What mattered now was marriage, a new life, new possibilities, the future.

Michael and I were married in September 1950 in a progressive synagogue in London. The subsequent ceremony was a strange one, in which I felt compelled to make a speech and thank my 'guardians', the Scotts, for preparing the wedding reception which according to my husband's family was disgraceful. The tables were not overflowing with masses of food as was usually the custom at Jewish weddings. I was very happy because I expected little and was grateful for anything. Michael's grandmother however who worshipped the ground her favourite grandson walked on, thought otherwise.

Another new chapter of my life has now began. [1950]

Michael was offered a job in Israel as a food technologist and asked to design and set up a hydrolisate plant in Telma, a food manufacturing factory in Haifa. Our honeymoon was the trip to the Holy Land with, en route, a short trip to Paris.

Israel in the 50's was a special place. A country which had recently won it's independence and, for many, fulfilled a biblical promise. Many Jews in the diaspora felt they could hold their heads high because there now was a Jewish state. For me, personally, the feeling of being in Israel was less euphoric. My aunts and uncles who emigrated from Poland when I was a child did welcome us but they were strangers to me as was my grandmother, on my father's side, who was still alive and living there. I could not help my private thoughts - why did they not try a bit harder to get us out from the hell!

This was not fair since I subsequently learned they tried hard to persuade my father to leave Poland and go to Israel. he refused. My father was a Marxist and not a Zionist, he could not forsee a future for himself in Israel and nor did he forsee what was about to happen in Poland.

Learning the language was the first task facing us. We went to an 'Ulpan' to learn Hebrew. It was like going back to school and becoming a child again except this time it was with one's husband. Despite the frustrations of learning a new language from a Bulgarian teacher who did not know a word of English, it was fun. Our class included many different nationalities all eager to acquire the new skill. I was very much aware of the fact that Jews who came from the many different countries ie. Romania, Hungary, Germany, Poland, Russia, France and USA etc brought with them the characteristics of their respective countries so you may well ask, since none of them were religious, what is a Jew?

We became friendly with a group of young American scientists mainly physicists who were invited to work in the Haifa Technical College. They were happy to leave their homeland where MacCarthy had declared war on anyone expressing liberal views and where they could be hounded for un-American activities and indeed several were. We also met singers and song writers who were busy composing 'folk' materials which we tried it out in various parties. We were growing up, still in our 20's, in a very exciting social and political climate. There was a sense of sharing, of not caring about material comforts and of warm frendships. I enjoyed dancing the Hora, I liked singing the folk songs, it was the closest I ever came to identifying myself with a tribe of a new nation finding itself, a tower of Babel, learning to live together.

I am writing this in the 90's looking back at the 50's Eastern Europe is on the verge of collapse because of a burgeoning wave of nationalism. Men everywhere seem to cling to their tribes, to their Gods, ready to die and to kill for their beliefs. I have experienced the ease with which we can assume the mantle of nationalism and how important it is to see the dangers and to guard against them. I am much more cynical about this now since I despise the kind of nationalism that leads to fundamentalism. Enough of philosophising for the time being.

I cherish many wonderful memories of Israel at that time. I was sorry to leave the many good friends I made there, in particular a beautiful American dancer with whom I had joined forces and who introduced me to the Martha Graham technique. Graham was then regarded as the most powerful priestess of modern dance. Rina, an American dancer, myself and an Yemenite dancer, Avi, formed a small group which toured and performed in many Kibbutzim, the agicultural settlements which proliferated at that time.

On one occasion we drove to an old established Kibbutz near an Arab border where we stayed overnight. We performed on a huge dining room floor with tables cleared for the purpose. There was a great sense of elation and a feeling that we were contributing to the culture and bringing something new to the community. I remember one incident clearly; wanting to go to the toilet in the middle of the night I had to be escorted there by a soldier with a machine gun who stood outside the outdoor toilet whilst I completed my task. It was, I thought at the time, a distinction of a sort. The borders had to be defended but there was then some hope that the the Jews and Arabs will reach some sort of agreement.

I was sorry to leave Israel although I never felt enough of a Zionist to want to stay there for the rest of my life.

Another chapter of my life came to an end.

After five years in Israel Michael was transfered back to England. And about the same time a number of our American friends returned to the States.

Our next port-of-call was Liverpool, fortunately only for 6 months. The northerners are lovely and friendly people but after the blue skies of Israel, the constant excitement, tension and dialogue, the sense of life on the edge, Liverpool seemed deathly dull.

Looking back at my life now I can tell you that each move though not easy and not always welcome was nevertheless a lesson in life.

After six months of Liverpool, Michael's job took us back to London where we found a large, damp and much neglected flat in a posh part of London, Knightsbridge near Brompton Oratory. It was here that I tasted more acutely the English class system. The house belonged to a titled lady, the widow of an Air Vice Marshall. She took some interest in me because although I was a foreigner she could not place me class-wise. I would be invited for tea to her sumptuous rooms upstairs. She never asked me too many questions and she never invited me with Michael whose name, Posner, clearly did not quite fit the protocol.

Just about that time Nancy Mitford had written a book based on the usage of U and Non-U language. Only in England are people judged by the accents and certain usage of vocabulary ie. If you come from the upper class you would say lavatory and if you come from the middle class you would say toilet!

We looked after Lady Morris's, cat whose name was Timothy. When eventually Timothy had to be put to sleep due to old age and illness, Lady Morris asked me to accompany her to her cottage in the country where we buried Timothy with great honour, putting his body in a small wooden coffin with flowers and shedding many tears.

It all seemed a bit strange to me at that time, thinking inwardly, even though I am a cat lover, that the English lavish more love on animals than human beings.

That was 1959, you see, and now we are in the 90's we seem to have lost even the love for animals, when we hear of so many cruelties and lack of care.

It was at this point that I began to think more seriously of a stage career. Yes, I wanted to act but I could still dance and as a dancer I did not have to worry about having a foreign accent. I managed to get an audition for a West End musical called Mr Venus and to my great suprise got the job. Shortly after this closed the marvelous musical, West Side Story, which combined entertainment with content opened in London and to be in a show like this became my ambition. There were auditions for a replacement English cast and I had a recall. However at the same time Michael informed me that our next move was going to be New Zealand where he had been offered a factory manager post. The greasepaint was well in my veins by now but I had to juggle my burgeoning stage career with my marriage. Brought up as I was to believe that my husband, the main bread winner, dictates the moves, I reluctantly had to accept the next move.

Before I proceed on with my next chapter I must confess to some blues and doubts creeping in, I am beginning to doubt the validity of writing all this down. Do you really want to listen? I am putting my mind in reverse, I am racing through the events, 'the bits and pieces of my life' where at the end of it I feel I have not really achieved all that much, so do you really want to hear? We love to read about the famous and the successful because it gives us hope, it elevates us from the mundane and we can vicariously identify with the heroes. Except who is to say who are the real heroes?

Marriage as we all know has its own ups and downs though I think I have been luckier than most. It is interesting now to look back from the view point of the 90's and see how much we have travelled not only in terms of gathering moss and getting older but to see how the changing social mores impinge on us and change our perceptions. We would like to think that we have individual minds and arrive at our attitudes because we thought things out for ourselves. I am referring here to the changing roles of the male/female relationships.

I, of course, wanted to have my cake and eat it too. I wanted the love and support of a husband which I craved and needed and the freedom to do my own thing. I feel I have only partially succeeded in this endeavour.

New Zealand 1960

We arrived in New Zealand in 1960. My first impression of the country was less than favourable. Geographically beautiful, culturally apparently a desert. I was not looking forward to my life there, boredom and being with people who did not share my interests were always two factors I feared most. An invitation, oneday, to a ladies luncheon confirmed my greatest fears. They were all friendly, dressed in flower-pattern frocks and white gloves. Their knowledge of children's illnesses, nappy rashes, fruit preserves and jam was astounding. I did not want to be here and I felt ungrateful and guilty for not being able to accept the cosy and easy life-style offered me on a platter. We bought a charming little house with 5/8th of an acre of garden, an unusual luxury. Michael was absorbed in his work, managing a food processing factory and I dreamed of dingy, smoked filled cafes, arty basements and intensive conversations about the meaning of art!

The unexpected did happen one day. I read in the local paper an announcement about a New Zealand poet who had arrived recently in Hastings and was to give a lecture in the local library on mythology, Jung and the Modern Man. Needless to say Michael and I went to the lecture not quite knowing what to expect. The lecture was quite electrifying. Louis Johnson, the poet, was a burly man with a handsome face looking more like a rugby player than a poet, but he spoke with great intelligence, sensitivity and humour.

I was a happily married young woman but the attraction to a man whose muse I became proved very powerful indeed. Louis also fulfilled a gap. A well-known New Zealand poet who showed such interest in me who spent many hours talking to me and instructing me in literature and art and encouraged me in my own creativity. We formed a literary society where other well known New Zealand poets and writers were invited to give talks and recitations. I too gave several recitals of movement and poetry. I became fascinated by the relationship of verbal images and physicality. I also became involved in various musical productions which I choreographed. My life in New Zealand became exciting.

At this time I developed a burning desire for motherhood. Wanting a child became almost an obsession. I wanted a family, I was ready for it and I knew that Michael and I would be wonderful parents. When at last my son was born on 25th May 1961 it was the happiest event in my whole life.

Today I am sitting in our comfortable home in Belsize Park in London. It is February 1994, 55 years since the tragic death of my parents. My son is 32 years old and I am crying my eyes out. My son has problems that I am going to tell you about later. In the meantime my son whom I love to distraction tells me that my anxiety about his well-being creates a very negative atmosphere at home, "why don't I just relax" he says. Why do his words hurt me so much? I am brought to thinking about my own parents and I miss them so much. If they lived their own natural life span they would not be probably alive by now. It all happened such a long time ago but I miss all those years growing up without them.

Holland 1962-3

We left New Zealand when our son Jeremy was 2 years old. I was quite happy to turn a new chapter. Michael's job now took us to Holland, not again a country of my choice but I was very absorbed in motherhood and did not greatly mind where we were. Holland is a strange mixture, very progressive on one hand, the first country to have gay clubs to which one could be escorted by a policeman, on the other hand, women stay at home with window boxes full of flowers, clean floors and polish door handles. I taught dance at the Rotterdam Dance Academy and Michael's spiritual quest found some outlet in meeting some people involved with Pak Subud, an Indonesian guru who introduced a practise called the Latihan, a meditation technique to help one tap into sources of energy and to become a more integrated being. We had been introduced to this in new Zealand by Louis Johnson and friends. My own attitude to the various spiritual quests has always been ambiguous. I have a great desire for self-improvement be it spiritual or intellectual and I tend to put those people on pedestal who seem to have attained the 'higher level' of awareness only to be disappointed by their behaviour because I expect them to be saints. There is, alas, a lot of spiritual 'fascism' about. People who seem to think that when they have found 'their' God or their way, it is THE only God or THE only way and here I part company.

London 1963-76

The two years in Holland passed quickly and we soon found ourselves packing again and preparing for our return to London.

After a short stay in Surbiton we moved to a rather 'yuppy' area in Weybridge, Surrey. I felt a bit out of place with my neighbours, young and upwardly mobile 'organisation-men', husbands and their conservatively liberal wives, a bit like us!! By now I had grown used to being an outsider wherever I found myself. I resumed my dance career by intensive work with the London Contemporary Dance Company and after a year of hard work I was asked to teach the Graham technique and eventually graduating to being a company member. I was never technically brilliant as a dancer but I did have what is called a 'stage presence; and I considered myself very lucky to have come thus far.

Michael was now working for J.Lyons in a senior managerial capacity. We moved to a bigger town house in Chiswick and Jeremy attended a progressive school near by. During school holidays I would take him to my dance classes, sitting him in the corner with a book or a toy. It was there that Jeremy met Jon K. an American percussionist who would sometimes accompany our dance classes. Jon was very much a product of the 60's a free spirit, interested in various Eastern philosophies, pot smoking, soft spoken, long haired young man for whom the drums and rhythms they could create provided universal truths. Needless to say Jeremy was hooked and declared that he wanted to become a drummer. As parents we were also imbued with the 60's syndrome of freedom of choice for children and 'do what ever makes you happy' attitude. We were therefore very willing to offer necessary tuition which Jon the drummer was eager to provide.

I remember writing to my aunt in Poland that Jeremy showed great interest and some skills in becoming a drummer. A response came by return telling me that this was not a profession to be taken seriously and I should definitely and strongly discourage it. I did want Jeremy to go to a University, his interest in reading books on Greek and Roman mythology was quite unusual for a boy of his age however he was far from numerate. According to various tests at the Tavistock Clinic this might have been due to the fact that his father was so good in this area or it was an emotional block or genetic inheritance from his mother, a guilt I secretly harboured'. No doubt, however, that Jeremy was a highly sensitive and intelligent boy who could express himself well.

Life in Chiswick seemed to flow effortlessly. I was busy dancing and performing at the Place, the home of the London Contemporary Dance Company, as well as teaching movement for actors at RADA and LAMDA. It was here working with actors that I realised that acting was what I wanted to do all along but never had the guts to admit it. I was still a member of the Company. Life was full and busy though not always fulfilling. Jeremy attended a progressive Quaker school in Letchworth, Hertfortshire and Michael became involved in the Gurdieff Movement and the Way of the Sufis through the work of J.G.Bennett in Coombe Springs where the philosophy was studied and practised. I, too, have a great need to believe in something beyond ourselves. Organised religion, however, does not interest me since it seems to seperate us rather than unite us. More wars have been fought in the name of God, so I would rather suffer the slings and arrows of outrageous paganism than profess to believe in goodness and love and not live according to this doctrine, which alas so many practitioners of various faiths seem to do. Why do I want an ideal world, there is no such thing.!

I despised the so-called typical middle-class world but I was very much a part of it and I became even more so when we moved yet again to a new flat in Hampstead. I played the charming hostess role to the hilt giving candle-lit dinner parties and occasionally coming across some fascinating people.. This semi-idyllic existence came abruptly to an end when Michael announced one day that he had been made redundant. I was teaching at RADA at the time and choreographing a show in Leeds.

Let me digress here for a minute; thinking of this time now in the 90s I can hardly believe that I have done all these things. I danced, I taught, I choreographed and now I am a struggling actress and my past matters not a jot but more of it later.

For the first time in my married life we were facing an uncertain future. Michael usually moved from one job to the next under the safe umbrella of a big corporation, so it felt like the safety blanket had been pulled from under our feet. The first thing we did was to remove Jeremy from the fee- paying school and put him in a Comprehensive School in Hamstead. The move was not an ideal step in his educational development but we felt we had no choice. Michael started to look for another job preferably in another field. He was fed up with industry and expressed his wish to use his skills in something more closely linked to human resources. Luckily an opportunity came for a job in UNICEF at their headquarters in New York. It all sounded most exciting. The interview went well and Michael was offered the job of Deputy Director of Personal Administration in UNICEF. Another page of my life was about to turn.

New York 1976-82

Packing, leaving the flat, saying goodbyes to my friends and my jobs and for me again moving into the unknown. I did not realise what an impact this move was to have on Jeremy who was then 15, just on the verge of adolescence. Michael seemed jubilant about his new job and excited about New York which he found less stuffy, more energised and full of vitality. His enthusiasm was catching and I too embraced New York with all my heart. Occasionally I found the culture-shock quite a jolt having got used to a more gentle rhythm of life in London. The main objective for me was to find a niche for myself as I did not wish to be just a wife of an UN official.

The group of friends who we first encountered, 25 years previously, in Israel and who all subsequently returned to the USA provided our basic social contact. They became our family. We shared our youth with them and here in our middle years we were able to re-establish our friendship. Americans or more precisely, New Yorkers, are easy to make contact with. There seems to be an instantaneous welcoming and openness, which for a newcomer suffering from culture-shock or home sickness is like a balm to an open wound. I slowly began to realise that though my future was yet unknown I was shedding an outer layer of self protection which gave me a certain sense of freedom.

It is strange how on reflection we realise certain things only by comparison to something else. I never realised until we lived in New York to what extent I have not denied but supressed my Jewishness simply because I never talked about it. In New York people are curious, they want to know where you come from, how and why you came to be here etc. and this is never regarded as an invasion on privacy which it would be in England. New York is a place where the best and the worst aspects of humanity inhabit the same place, beauty and vulgarity, poverty and riches, aggression and gentleness, anything and everything which is human.

New York is also a place where, after 2 weeks of living there, you can feel like a native. I began to enjoy many bizzare encounters and chats with people I met in cafes or museums. People who were only too willing to talk about the complexities of their lives, who wear their hearts on their sleeves.

I began teaching movement at the Julliard School's drama department, while attending acting classes at Uta Hagan studio and eventually I was offered a place at Hunter College to do an MA in Theatre Arts. I at last had a structure which I always needed and life was again rolling on.

In my determination to 'make a go' of it I did not perhaps realise that the New York experience was not having the same effect on my son.

It is only in retrospect I now know what the trauma of moving meant for my son. No friends and a cultural ethos where it is OK to be aggressive in order to be noticed let alone survive was an anathema to Jeremy who is by nature non-aggressive and non competitive.

He stayed at home for the first few weeks refusing to leave his room.

It is a cliche to say that there is only one kind of unconditional love and that is the mother's love for her child and yet how many mistakes, wittingly or unwittingly, we make in the name of that love. When finally Jeremy started going to school but not working very hard I said many awful things that I realised later may have made a profound impression on him. I said things like "I never had the opportunities you have, why are you not taking the advantages laid for you at your feet?" How was I to know in saying that, I may have created a guilt with which he could not cope. The more I tried the less responsive he became. I wanted closeness, friendship and trust at the same time as I threw accusatory remarks at him. I invested those feelings in my son and only now I know that he had no right to be on the receiving end of them. Jeremy had a natural sense of rebelliousness against authority and was prone to subversive behaviour. I can see now this was his own way of asserting himself. Was I secretly proud of it? Did I encourage it? Did I see my son as a high- spirited individual daring to be a nonconformist whilst I had to be an obedient girl to gain love and attention?

Even today I cannot answer these questions.

My son's nonconformist behaviour reached a danger point when he began to associate with friends, mainly musicians, much older than himself. He veered towards the counter-culture writers like William Burroughs who made a deep impression on him, as well as the works, he much admired, of Beaudalaire and especially Dostoyevski's, 'Notes from Underground' Slowly but surely he began to withdraw into a world of his own. I was beginning to lose contact, attributing certain behavioural characteristics to adolescence. What sometimes hurt deeply was the occasional look of hostility when he was confronted.

It was at that time that we received a call from the NY Police informing us about Jay's whereabouts. He was picked up down town New York trying to buy methadone from a' pusher' The Police were apparently more interested in catching the 'pusher' but seeing a new boy walking in a neighbourhood to which, in the words of the Cop, he did not belong they decided to take him in for questioning.

Michael went with Jeremy to the Night Court and a short trial and sentencing he was released, with a warning and lecture from the sympathetic policeman who arrested him.

The problem of addiction is such that Jeremy thought he had everything under control, did not understand what the fuss was all about and in his eyes he was not do anything wrong.

We did however manage to persuade him to go to a psychologist as his school work began to suffer and he was threatened with expulsion. The verdict of the examination was that Jeremy was in a great deal of emotional pain, something I found so difficult to understand.

Soon after the visit to the psychologist a thunderbolt came from heaven or so it felt. When making my son's bed and turning over the mattress I found a syringe. My knowledge of drugs was limited to what I read in the press but I knew it signified something destructive. When I confronted him with my discovery I quickly accepted the excuse "......well it was only a stupid experiment never to be repeated again". I later recognised I did not want to believe the implications of what I discovered; I too was in denial. Again and again, in my mind, I go back to this incident and many other similar incidents that followed.

Shortly after the syringe discovery Jeremy formed a relationship with Joan, a woman some 6 years older than him. She looked dirty and unappetising but she wrote poetry, loved William Burroughs' books, quoted Ginsberg and Jeremy was completely under her spell and felt very protective of her. Joan was a heroin addict which I did not know at the time but even if I had known there was nothing I could do. Jeremy assured me that she did have a problem but she was on methadone programme which was the best cure. Joan, as I later discovered, was forging prescriptions and stealing money to obtain drugs and my then not-so-street-wise son assured me that he was trying to help her. By this time he lost total interest in school and no amount of persuasion could change this course. We felt completely helpless and I remember thinking this was just a nightmare that will pass. Joan was placed in a clinic by her parents and Jeremy helped her to escape, insisting that the treatment she was receiving was inhuman, brutal and totally wrong for her condition. What I did not know was that he was planning to help her abscond without telling anyone. It was only when the head of the clinic contacted the police who in turn called us that we realised what happened. He did not return home and Michael and I were quite desperate with fear. After all this was

New York, the papers were full of stories of young people raped, murdered, drugged and abandoned. After two agonising days of no news Jeremy phoned to say that he and Joan were in Boston and they were fine. He put up such a convincing and logical argument explaining why Joan had to leave this terrible place that I almost believed him and part of me felt quite proud that he had the guts to do it.

Now I know that the more desperate one is the more one wishes to believe in whatever seems more comforting, denial again!.

Jeremy said that he would like to come home but Joan had to come with him. I agreed to this minor blackmail and would have agreed to anything so long as he came home.

And so began a short spell of hell. Joan's mother called to say that Joan is a lost cause that she was so heavily into drugs and that her influence on my son might lead to disaster and that we should not allow the relationship to continue for his sake. How were we supposed to pull them apart? Again my clever son persuaded me that Joan's family did not understand the problem and that what Joan needed was support and love. If I were to write a book on the subject of living with an addict I would entitle it 'Love is not enough'.

Let me tell you what the hell consisted of. We seldom had an uninterrupted night. Jeremy and Joan did not sleep, they listened to strange music all night long. The room in which they lived looked like a refugee camp after some deluge. There were cigarette burns in the carpet, the settee, the curtains and bed linen, there was candle wax on the floor and the untidiness and dirt beyond belief. Well may you ask, how we did put up with it. We wanted our son close to us, with no other close family and we felt guilty for uprooting him and we wanted to believe that it would pass......

Today, January 1995 I watched a programme on TV about some Holocaust survivors telling their horrific stories. One woman, a mother of a 39 year old son, lived through an unimaginable nightmare. Ridden with typhoid she was lying under a pile of bodies, it was the day that the Germans capitulated she heard some footsteps and with the last remaining strength she started calling out. The Russian liberators heard her faint cries and following the sound of her voice dug her out from under that pile of dead bodies.

Many years later her son came to realise what she had been through. He now visits her once a month and calls her twice a week. There was a clip of this now 65 year old mother greeting her son as he came to visit her "Oh there is my angel" she said. I was very envious of this mother. On reflection I understand that what happened in my family was different, I was not the victim anymore my son became the victim. I also realise that the demands we, we the survivors, put on our children can be damaging. Since the family becomes the only safe-haven when the faith in others becomes eroded we place huge demands and expectations on our children's shoulders.

Joan continued to have an impossible strong hold on Jeremy and although they split up for a short time, she came back. The sense of helplessnes was overwhelming and a cloud of sadness hung over us continually. I tried as much as possible to busy myself with my work. I continued teaching at the famous Julliard School, I worked for my Masters degree and sought acting jobs wherever possible. We could no longer tolerate Joan and Jeremy living with us and forced the issue. Joan found a small apartment near Harlem. She assured us that she wanted to return to college and that this would be the best solution for the time being. Jeremy insisted in going with her. It took us many hard blows to realise that one should never trust an addict not because they are evil, they lie because they cannot help it, it is part of the illness of addiction. We did not know this at the time partly because we were in denial of the problem and partly because we were at a loss to know what else to do. A common symptom when living with an addict.

They move out; we could not persuade Jeremy to stay. We still hoped that it would pass and that our support will show them that at least we cared. Michael and I would often take bags of food and deliver them at the doorstep of Joan and Jeremy's apartment. One thing which they managed to do in their constant drugged state was a lot of reading. Most of it was the counter- culture subversive literature of some nevertheless good writers like William Burroughs whom they actually met at a Methadone clinic where Burroughs would go regularly to receive his dose of heroin substitute.

Both Joan and Jeremy had good minds and high intelligence and it was so tragic to see that their abilities were not be put to better use.

Even in Jeremy's field of music where he showed so much talent, he did manage to get himself involved with various groups and sometimes I would get a call from a leader of such a group telling me that Jeremy was wasting his talent that he was unreliable, did not turn up for rehearsals and that they had to let him go. Jeremy when confronted with this scenario always managed to find something which would prove how unjust such accusations were. He too was in denial.

I enjoyed living in New York. We had wonderful friends, I was constantly busy, working or learning and despite various problems at work, Michael was enjoying the UN and the challenge that the work presented. We often talked about Jeremy with our friends who also had problems with their children and we decided that maybe this was the result of the 60's more liberal approach to education, a belief to which I strongly subscribed but was reluctant to use as an excuse. We just constantly hoped that Jeremy would grow out of it. We will never know exactly the extent of the problem and what Jeremy must have gone through to obtain drugs. We noticed a few missing items; an expensive Swiss watch which Michael had bought for my birthday, items of clothing, a camera, a ring etc. When confronted there was such pain of disbelief in Jeremys' eyes. He had the ability to make me feel guilty for even having such thoughts and on our part it was easier to believe in some thief or intruder than accept the fact of one's son doing the thieving. Such is the power of denial.

Year in Brandeis

I applied for a job at Brandeis University in Boston was interviewed and offered it. I needed to get away and I needed to taste my independence. I taught movement for actors in the Theatre Department, choreogrphed musicals and was even given a play to direct. I was intoxicated with the sense of achievement. It was not easy to get a job at an American University, my title was Professor Posner and my work there was very much appreciated by the head of the department, Ted Kazanoff, and by the students. I made a number of friends, went to many lectures and had a fascinating and stimulating time.

They did ask me to stay on for another year but Michael was beginning to tire of his weekly visits to Boston and I thought it was time to come home! Also Michael's job with UNICEF in New York came to an end and he was offered a transfer to the UNICEF office in Denmark, Copenhagen.

I was sad to leave New York but we had no option. We had become accustomed to a certain standard of living so leaving the security of the UN and looking for other jobs in a highly competitve American market at the age of 50 was not an alternative. Jeremy refused to come with us and decided to stay in New York with Joan. The struggle continued. We sought some help from a prominent psychiatrist who advised us to leave him. At the age of 19 he should be able to begin to take responsibility for himself which is one thing that in my heart of hearts I knew he was incapable. Also the meaning of responsibility does not feature in the addict's vocabulary except for achieving the next fix. However we listened to the experts and anyway we could not force him to come with us nor did we feel we could leave him entirely without any support. So we found an apartment for him for which we paid rent in advance and begged him not to let Joan move in. Michael also found him a job in UNICEF's greeting card department.

Me and my Father, W arsaw ca 1938

My Mother, Me, my aunt Regina and my Father, Warsaw ca 1938

My aunt Lola

Lola's children   Oleg   Roma

Me in Polish National costume
aged   ca 8

Squadron

Leader Sydney Scott
1945

Sophie, Me and Edith in the hostel
ca 1946

Me at Haifa Beach ca 1952

Michael and Me, Haifa ca 1953

Jeremy aged 6 months and Me ,
New Zealand ca 1961

Jeremy, Weybridge ca 1966

Jeremy and Zac, London ca 1965

Jeremy ca 1994

Me & Lola, Warsaw 1996

Jeremy ca1997

Zac in his first school uniform 2000

**Me & Michael
Golden Wedding 2000**

Me as Queen Lear
in The Yiddish Queen Lear, 2001

Zac and Me, London 2011

Me and Michael 2012

Copenhagen 1982-84

We went to Copenhagen with a heavy heart. My feelings of deja-vu persisted yet again. We were not particularly interested in large houses outside the city where so many of the UN officials were based. Michael found a charming flat on 4th. floor walk-up with a lot of character in the old part of central Copenhagen. I was again faced with the reality of being a foreigner in a land where I could not speak the language, where I did not know anyone and where the prospects of work were not very promising. The greatest fear always I have had had was being an idle together with other wives who were forever complaining and arranging boring cocktail parties. However after a few lonely weeks I discovered some interesting possibilities. I found work with the English Speaking Theatre in Denmark and with another theatre company run by an English woman who was married to a Dane. We put on a very popular version of Robinson Crouse with strong political under-tones of the third world and the Imperialistic power.

As far as Jeremy was concerned I felt I was living on top of an unexploded bomb waiting to go off any minute. Sure enough a letter arrived from the landlord in whose house Jeremy was living, telling us that Joan who had clearly moved in, was causing a lot of trouble, creating disturbances by shouting and appearing stoned most of the time. If this continued he would be forced to evict both of them. I immediately wrote a frantic letter to Joan's father begging him to remove Joan from the scene. Michael was shortly going to New York and was to persuade Jeremy to come and live with us in Copenhagen. My nights were full of bad dreams and constant worries. I tried to tell myself that Jeremy had intelligence, talent and given the knowledge that he was loved no matter what, sooner or later he would see the LIGHT.

During his visit to New York Michael made a deal with Jeremy. We knew his relationship with Joan was faltering and Michael begged him to come and live with us in Copenhagen and that we would do everything in our power to make his life comfortable. To our great suprise he agreed on one condition. He needed methadone as he was now physiologically addicted and could not manage life without it. Michael promised him that he would arrange this. We were so happy to have him with us we would have said yes to anything. Jeremy agreed to come for Xmas. We bought him a return ticket and waited at the airport for him to arrive wondering if he actually was on the plane. He was, he was actually the last off the plane! He stayed one week during which time he met a Danish girl, Annette, and wanted to stay. He agreed to go back to New York, clear his flat and return. Denmark is a liberal country especially to any form of so-called deviant social behaviour, prepared to listen to a problem without being too judgmental. And so it was that a Danish doctor to the UN staff on hearing the problem was reluctantly prepared to prescribe the needed dosage of methadone despite the fact that in Demark, methadone is a class A drug and not usually approved.

Our son was back with us. As I have already told you many times his gift for persuasive talk was quite phenomenal. Well read but not conventionally well educated and now age 21 he could put up a very convincing argument for the legalisation of drugs. In retrospect I now see that this was a problem for us. He could sound so rational that even though I did not entirely agree with him I had to concede that he was entitled to his point of view.

Now, many years later, I agree with some of his views. Drugs should be legalised but strictly controlled and governments in each country should invest in, Rehab centres for those ready to benefit from such treatments. Addiction should be treated as a form of illness.

However back to Denmark and Jeremy's promises that he will give up drugs when he is ready sounded by now quite familiar.

I had to get on with my own life, to make some sense of it all. I was given a part in a play with an English Speaking Theatre Company as well as some teaching which saved my life. Most of the other UN wives took to stiff gins and occasional outings which I would have found most frustrating but I have a feeling I have told you this before.

Jeremy in the meantime found some musicians and started to play some gigs. Having attended such events I noticed that the other young people were in similar states of being, not so much from drugs as alcohol. Jeremy with his new girl friend Annette, a sweet and pretty looking girl who seemed to accept him and love him, found some accommodation although he was still totally dependent on us financially.

I remember during that time my aunt, Lola, visiting us in Copenhagen. Lola was not a person one could discuss problems with. In her world everything was ordered and disciplined. I pretended that things were fine. Occasionally, I tried to make her aware of the fact that the world had changed and that parents were no longer all- powerful and that there were outside forces bearing more influence on young people than ever before. Whatever I said fell on stony ground and she made me feel guilty for allowing my son to choose his friends, his clothes and the things he most loved to do. I found these accusations unbearably painful recognising a grain of truth in them but realising the hopelessnes and powerlessnes in the situation.

Two years in Denmark passed very quickly however I wanted to return to a country where everyone spoke the language with which I was most familiar, so it was with much relief I learned that Michael had also had enough of exile and was looking forward to coming back to London.

Jeremy however decided to stay in Copenhagen. He had his girlfriend his music and methadone and seemed very much at homUnder the Danish law peoplc who live in the country without a job for more than three months are obliged to leave the country and there were increasing difficulties in officially obtaining methadone. Knowing this we could leave him for the time being, go to London find a place to live and take it from there.

London 1985 on

Thus to another new chapter in our lives.

London!! Back ,'home' We found a nice large flat in Belsize Park, a very desirable location, although I would rather live in one room and exchange the luxury for the certainty of my son's health. It was here that we joined the Family Anonymous organization and started attending meetings regularly. These are run on the basis of self-help groups with a 12 step programme developed from Alcoholics Anonymous. I am not by nature attracted to any groups that have a slightly evangelical flavour but my need was stronger than any negative judgment I might have. One enormous comfort I derived from the groups was shedding my sense of guilt. Whatever I did I was not responsible for my son becoming an addict. There were people in the groups from many different backgrounds ie. possessive parents, strict parents, working class parents, middle and upper class parents from all economic levels and sometimes children or partners of addicts. They all had the same problems they too were all addicts, addicted to their addicts. We were all caught in the same predicament. We all suffered from a cocktail of anxiety, impotence in the face of the problem, anger, fear, guilt and constant frustration. One of the most important aspects of the FA doctrine I learnt is that of

Tough Love, putting the responsibility for their lives on the addict and making a clear distinction between the fact that one wishes to help the addict but not the illness. The illness is the responsibility of the addict and only he or she is in the position to change this.

Jeremy arrived from Denmark with Annette both looking sick. We tried to make it clear that we were not ready or willing to accept his behaviour any longer, that help was possible and we were no longer willing to be manipulated or supportive except in helping him to get better. We believed this could be achieved if he would enter a rehabilitation clinic. After much hard talk Jeremy agreed to go. Our joy and happiness was short lived. After only two weeks he discharged himself saying he was not ready. We were wasting our money and that he had to do it his own way.

Back on the marry-go-round. We were religiously attending the FA meetings, our only source of support. In the meantime Jeremy found a room in which to live and our contact with him became tenuous.

To follow a set of rules which are contrary to all of one's instincts feels like stepping into hell and numbing oneself to the surrounding fires. I was trying hard to establish myself as an actress which at my age and with a slight foreign accent was not easy but keeping busy seemed like taking pain killers to stop the pain from consuming my whole being. Michael and I talked about the situation constantly and it is fortunate that we could talk althought we did not always agree. I am, by nature, pro-active and see problems as something to be solved though I do not always know how. Michael takes the attitude that there is often nothing one can do and that one has to accept one's helplesness. One feels one must do something if one only knew what! Despite the fact that I could see the rational I was not always able to apply its logic. We lived in constant fear that something drastic might happen and there was nothing we could do to prevent it. The result, a constant tight band round ones head and a stone in ones stomach.

One night it did happen. The phone rang at about 3 am. I jumped out of bed with a pounding heart. Jeremy was living in the house of a friend and it was his mother who called. Jeremy was in hospital. He had fallen out of 2nd. storey window, his condition was not yet properly diagnosed. We got to the hospital feeling both horror and numbness. I also felt anger and clung to that feeling because the emotion of anger helped me to keep my sanity. Why did he inflict this on himself? There was no answer to that question.

We were told by the nurse that he was not yet fully conscious and that they did not as yet know the full effect of the damage. He had several broken bones including a skull fracture. It was hoped there was little damage internally or to the spine. I remember trembling inwardly, picturing my son in a wheel chair for the rest of his life. We had to inform the hospital of his addiction problem because if he was suddenly deprived of methadone he might have a seizure. We stayed until he regained consciousness and such is the power of the addiction illness that the very first words he managed to utter were,"I need some methadone" and then later by way of reassurance,"It's not what you think, it's not the drugs I just lost my balanc"

I looked down at the thin broken body of my beautiful son and again the mixture of love, pity and powerful anger were overwhelming. Jeremy made a remarkable physical recovery but mentally and spiritually he was deeply scarred though still able to put up a strong defense for his chosen life style.

After many discussions and arguments with both of us, including a shouting match over several hours in the hospital's exercise room, he agreed to go to another Treatment Centre run on the principle of the 12 step AA programme. The sense of relief and hope was indescribable though I had learned by then that life was to be lived one day at the time, a good

AA dictum.   I was reminded again of my own childhood but all the pain of my past faded into insignificance and I thought how much harder it is to face problems in isolation to the rest of the society.

Whatever I have been through as a child not only happened to me but to millions of others. Not much consolation at the time but here we were trying to cope with and face our own problems. Every day Jeremy spent in the recovery centre was a bonus day.   Michael who learnt some buddhist breathing exercises helped me in the technique of relaxation. We were gathering our strength and bracing ourselves for any eventualities.

After 3 weeks in the recovery programme we had a   phone   call   from   Jeremy's   counsellor informing us that Jeremy had left the clinic and that unless he showed a 100% commitment to his recovery he was wasting his time. I felt the familiar band tightening on my forehead. The only advice the counsellor could offer was not to assist Jeremy in anyway hoping that the difficult situation he will inevitably find himself in will point him in the right direction. He now knows that help is possible.

When we are forced to do something which goes contrary to human instinct we tread into an abyss of despair; that is the only way I can describe what followed. When Jeremy finally showed up he was still hobbling on crutches and looking much distressed, made worse by his uniform of black homburg and floor-length black leather German army greatcoat! I had to brace myself since my natural instinct was to put my arms around him and tell him that everything will be fine. He must have sensed this as he proceeded pushing all my emotional buttons. "I am a human being and I am entitled to my choices. Yes, I am an addict and I should be allowed to deal with my problems in my own way. But please don't turn me away"

What I did now was the hardest thing with which any mother was ever faced. The action I took was against every natural instinct in my body. I knew, however, if I weakened he would never return to the clinic and so I said that although I recognised his freedom of choice, I did not wish to be drawn into his sickness and if he wished to do this on his own he would have to do it without our assistance and with this I shut the door on him. Tough Love!!

How inadequate are the words to describe our emotions. I felt a physical pain in the pit of my stomach but I knew I did the right thing. Jeremy hobbled away and I shall never forget the expression on his face. I do not know where he went or where he spent the night but next day he reappeared resolved to go back to the recovery centre and phoned his counsellor to persuade her to readmit him, which she finally did. Such is the power of the addiction that when finally Michael took him to Canterbury by car Jeremy changed his mind several times and Michael had to stop the car en-route and offer to let him get out. Miraculously they arrived at the clinic and to our great relief Jeremy stayed there for two more months.

I guess it was not always easy for him, but he clearly persevered. At the end of the two months he was a changed person, bright, open and cheerful though still a bit critical of the 12 step system. We talked to some of the friends he made there and it was rewarding to hear how helpful to others Jeremy had become. One young man, in particular, told us that Jeremy was one of the reasons why he decided to stay on at the clinic and get 'clean'.

A short period followed in a half way house which in retrospect was not enough. Not much was done to prepare the recovering addicts to resume their shattered lives beyond daily group therapy sessions.

Addicts like alcoholics are recommended to attend regular weekly meetings for a protracted period.

It was at one of those meetings that Jeremy met a beautiful girl with similar problems. Neither of them were ready for an emotional involvement and the relationship did not last long but Jeremy seemed more capable now of dealing with life.

Both Michael and I felt we had regained our son. We could laugh again; we could cry; we could talk and even whe sometimes disagreeing with him I had to acknowledge his point of view which was always thoughtful if unconventional.

I must also confess that I still hoped that Jeremy might now be interested in going to college to make-up for the lost time. He certainly had a good brain, was well read and this seemed like a good opportunity. There was nothing to stop him now but after a few attempts at discussing such possibilities I realised that I had to back off. Jeremy was involved in musicwhich is what he loves best and so he returned to his first love.

Being a handsome and charming young man he was hardly ever without female company. One day, Jeremy introduced me to his new girl friend, G. One thing my son taught me was that it was not imperative for me to like his girl friends but if one did it was a real bonus and so for a while I did like G and tried hard not to be too judgmental.

For a while life seemed to be moving in the right direction, the most important thing being we had our son, we could talk again, joke again, the dark clouds had lifted from our heads, the band around our heads loosened. I even got into the establishment theatre and for 7 months worked with the RSC in a play called 'The Dybbuk' I was also doing some teaching and life seemed good and full. In the summer and for five years running I had a prestigious summer job teaching in Oxford. I want to recount a little story here which will seem to you like bragging but which was so nice for me to hear. I have never told this to anyone before.

One day a student said to me ,"How can I put it into words it sounds so banal but I want to know how you get your energy, this life force? You make me feel that growing old is OK. Looking at you one senses eternal youth" I do not know why I remember this now but it was one of the most wonderful compliments I ever had.

When life seems full to the brim there is a little fatalist within me that says 'watch out it can not last for ever' Nothing lasts for ever. I was beginning to hear stories I would rather not have heard. G, I noticed, was trying to justify herself all the time. She told me her terrible family history; a father she hardly knew who left home leaving her mother in dire circumstances. She also had a very destructive relationship with her mother who apparently was a pot-smoking middle-aged-hippy. When G finally traced her father he was living with another woman and their children and would not see her, shutting the door in her face. I never will know whether the story had any veracity since she was prone to dramatic interpretations of her life events. What bothered me much more was that I noticed her tendency to put people down and especially Jeremy of whom I must admit I felt very protective. I made the mistake of voicing my reservations to Jeremy and was immediately accused of middle class values. Not being English born the whole idea of class was an anathema to my way of thinking. I admired people who had sensitivity and a nobleness of spirit which had nothing to do with class. As I told you before, my desire for a family which I had never had was so strong I wanted a daughter-in-law, I wanted grandchildren and if my son found a woman who loved him and who he loved I would have been so happy. Jeremy and G would visit us quite often, it began to feel like a family. I tried to ignore the things about her which troubled me and every time a negative thought crept into my head I pushed it away telling myself 'so long as he is happy' it is not my business to interfere or be judgemental. One day they even mentioned marriage and I gave G a present an old ring which Michael had given to me many years before. This seemingly idyllic state did not last long.

I was shattered when G informed me that Jeremy had relapsed. He was taking drugs again and when confronted he exploded, G had betrayed him. I was in a way thankful because I was beginning to suspect this but thought maybe it was my paranoia - it is always better to know or is it?. I just knew that I could not go through all this again. Jeremy as always was very eloquent; he admitted to a minor 'slip' nothing to worry about everything was under control, he could handle it!. The old habits come back so easily. I wanted to believe him and my denial was also a part of my survival kit.

I have truly learned I was powerless in these situations and the responsibility lay with my son. If only the last sentence also meant that one was not involved, that one could step out of the situation and let him get on with it. It is so hard or at least it is hard for me. Jeremy did go back to the recovery centre of his own free-will but did not stay there for long as he was going on tour with a band and that seemed to him to be more important than his recovery.

Michael and I just kept our fingers crossed. We went on with our lives and hoped for the best. After a while the pain created a numbing effect when we felt we could not take anymore and we carried on with life in a 'zombie' like state, not knowing what else to do to help. The tight bands around our heads returned. The guilt returned; what had we done that created this condition.

The worse was still to come. A phone call from G announcing that although she loved him very much, she had had enough and was throwing his things out of her flat and calling the police if he gave her any trouble. The torrential verbal outpouring of my eloquent son was something to behold. According to Jeremy, G was being grossly unreasonable. He still loves her and this is how she returned his love. This gave rise to tremendous anger after all he felt he had tried to do for her. All women in his eyes were bitches and he saw himself as the misunderstood victim. Needless to say Michael and I went to to help him pick up his belongings, some of which indeed were by now scattered on the street and with G standing there looking daggers at him. We brought our son back once again to the 'fold'. I can only tell you never to underestimate the problem of living with an addict. There are two distinct personalities inhabiting the body of each addict, well certainly in Jeremy. One is the person who is intelligent, sweet and sensitive and the other is the illness which is mean, selfish, self- absorbed, prone to lies and thievery. The addicts first love is the drug of choice. Jeremy did not stay with us for very long this time and we were not absolutely clear whether he was or was not using as his behaviour was quite amiable. He soon found a room in a shared household and we saw him from time to time when he chose to appear or need some financial assistance.

One day he announced that he met a girl in the pub where he was playing and that she was different to all these other women in his life. My heart missed a beat on hearing this because I knew he was still recovering from the G relationship although he acknowledged it's destructiveness. Thus L appeared one day and all my fears vanished immediately. L was a lovely young woman with a madonna-like face, delicate features and strong opinions. She seemed intelligent and was obviously very much in love with Jeremy. I embraced her as my own daughter partly in the hope she would help him through his problem. L seemed to have clicked with Michael which pleased me enormously as she was the first person in my son's life to whom Michael related. She was very interested in visual arts and had a no-nonsense approach to life. I thought she was more suspicious of me. I was only after all a struggling actress at the point she met me and I felt I appeared to her too theatrical. I honestly did not much care what she thought of me I was more concerned with my son's happiness and well-being. I later discovered that L came from a rather wealthy middle-class background against which she rebelled and sought to make her own way. She had given up quite a lucrative job though she had managed to buy her own flat and wanted to devote her time to more creative activities. Working as I do with so many young people I found nothing strange in those ambitions. Jeremy moved in with L and for a relatively short time seemed happy. I never asked if he was 'using', partly because it was no longer my business to know. That did not mean we were not anxious though in a way we did not want to know.

One day to my suprise and a sinking feeling at the pit of my stomach, yet again, Jeremy told me that he was finding living with L difficult she seemed possessive and that the flat was too small to contain their big emotions. I could not help being reminded of the many visits I paid to Eastern Europe where whole families lived in even more confined spaces but I tried very hard not to be judgmental. I was always prepared to listen to his problems and I must tell you, that in retrospect, I should have been less accommodating and strong enough to tell him to get on with his own life. Years of living with the addiction illness takes this kind of rationality away.

By now L was pregnant. I received the news with very mixed feelings. Part of me was overjoyed; I so wanted to be a grandmother and another part of me was so afraid aware of the unsteadiness of that relationship and what that could mean for a growing child. We could not offer advice; this was never asked for but we did offer some practical suggestions. I noticed, however, that L was not interested in our help. She was determined to have the child no matter what and on one occasion expressed to Michael her view that the notion of nuclear family is grossly exaggerated; all a child needs is his mother and that is that. Warning bells began to ring because on that issue I am old fashioned. I do not care what choices grown-up people make regarding their own lives. In my view, when it comes to children nothing replaces the mother- father combination even though we know how much misery there sometimes is in dysfunctional families. Jeremy started telling me again that L's demands of him were unreasonable. They discussed the situation of the child and he assured her that in the event of him moving out he would still be a good father and she assured him that he would always have access to the child.

Just at that time I was offered a job in the Edinburgh Fringe festival to play the role of a Grandmamma in an adaptation of Dostoyevski's novel,'The Gambler'. During the run on August14th.1995 I received a telegram announcing the birth of my grandson. Everyone in the company toasted me now that I became a real grandma. Full of excitement and trepidation I could not wait to get back to London. I went shopping as soon as I could and purchased all kinds of baby things. Michael called me from London and told me that Jeremy was beside himself with excitement proud to be a father and for a while I thought that maybe the responsibility he now had will help him to steady his life.

Finally we met L's parents in celebration of the birth and it felt like, at last, there was a semblance of a family something I always craved. It was alas not to be.   L and Jeremy's relationship quickly deteriorated.   I found myself supporting her at first since it was she who was now left with the emotional and practical turmoil of looking after the baby. I was again torn between my loyalty to my son and my confused state of mind.   Jeremy wanted my unreserved support which I was not always able to give.   I just wanted to be a normal grandma looking after and enjoying the baby whenever I could.   Zac seemed a beautiful child, an angel face and a calm disposition and my heart sank every time I looked at him fearing for his future.   Jeremy was visiting us more and more frequently telling us that life with L was becoming more and more impossible. L now seemed to turn her hostility on us and communication deteriorated   until   it became   non-existent. Since nothing ever stays still the rumblings were just a preparation for a big storm.   L's final outburst was throwing Jeremy out of her flat.

Here we go again!.   I ask you what would you do? Jeremy was in a terrible state he had nowhere else to go so of course we suggested that he came to live with us even though such an arrangement was far from ideal.   Jeremy, we now knew was on methadone, a prescription given to heroin addicts to get them off the streets and supposedly to steady them. However, as we learned subsequently methadone is far harder to get out of one's system than pure heroin.

So here we were back where we started. Jeremy talking again with his usual eloquence trying to convince us that this was the only way out for him at the moment although he was in the throes of a deep depression. Even with one's beloved son one does not always see 'the wood for the trees' with utmost clarity. We were back on the addiction with our addict with our guilt, anger, fear, impotence and lack of control. I only now understand the cause of his depression. He felt he had let himself down and he hated himself for that; but at the same time he was trying to find all the possible excuses even if it meant placing the blame outside himself. He was the victim, a 'worm' but a 'special worm'.

L in the meantime used the pretext of his addiction to withdraw access to the child from him and from us. I am not going to analyse the motives for such action because I do not fully understand them. Maybe it was the ultimate personal vendetta or maybe it was a rational decision on her part. I shall never know.

We managed subsequently after some wrangling, to make an arrangement to see Zac once a week. I was always under the impression that L was willing to accommodate us but she did not trust Jeremy.

Living with Jeremy in the state he was in was not a piece-of-cake, to put it mildly. Every morning I was faced with a young man who looked like he was on the verge of total collapse and yet again my feelings alternated between wanting to take him in my arms and wish all his troubles away and fury with him for letting his life and his problems so invade our lives. He was now 35 years old and we were badly in need of some respite from constant trauma and anxiety.

We did manage however to see Zac on a weekly basis and cherished the few hours of grandparenthood. Jeremy had all the qualities of being a good father but his changing moods were sometimes unpredictable. On one occasion he seemed to be paralysed by his son's visit and quite unable to cope. L and Jeremy could not breathe the same air anymore and on another occasion during their visit a 'vulcano' erupted. It was on my birthday L brought Zac and it was a joy to see him. It was obvious she wanted to stay and was reluctant to leave Zac with us. Out of the blue and for no reason, clear to me, Jeremy started screaming at L, one insult led to another. L picked Zac up saying "That is that, you will never see him again" This little scene propelled me out on to the street running wildly to and fro like a woman possessed. I knew this was indeed the end.

The family I always wanted and never had was on the brink of total collapse.

Since that incident I did not see my grandson for a long time and my son did not see his son ever again. Jeremy did not want me to interfere in his life and he did not want me to try and attempt some kind of reconciliation.

I did not see Zac for nearly 2 years. He was 3 years old in August and I have been deprived of the pleasure of taking him to his first pantomime, of buying him books, of learning about his interests or holding him and being grandma. Jeremy was not in the position to do anything about the situation either certainly not as long as he was on methadone and possibly in need of other drugs.

June 12th 1997 , Another Start

A cloudy and chilly day for this time of the year.

I am looking back over the last 2 years. Jeremy had nowhere else to go so he came to live with us, in a state of deep depression, the seriousness of which I did not realise at the time. I was also quite busy, rehearsing a play in a small theatre in Hampstead.

Jeremy stayed in bed most of the time, reading. If and when we talked the conversations were mostly one sided; it was Jeremy expressing his dark and negative view of life, with some of which, I have to say, I had to agree. Yes, there is less hope now for a better future; yes, most young people live with greater insecurities regarding their jobs if they are lucky enough to have them. And many of those who live on the dole have given up. I know the situation is far from rosy but I cannot stand it when it is also used as an excuse for inactivity and inertia.

My poor son did not seem able to change gear and find another direction. Not out of unwillingness, as I later discovered, but out of fear of not being able to 'make' it. He did have a short period of playing with a newly formed group in which he was highly regarded as a percussionist.

My son speaks well but his words hurt me.   I listen with amazement to the fluency of his speech but I cannot believe what he is saying "Why did you not ask me if I wanted to come to New York with you. I was15 years old I could have stayed in England", "But", I replied "we had no-one to leave you with. We are a small family and we believed that it was better that we should have stayed together". "You were overprotective of me, Mum. You did not let me grow up. I was so unhappy I resorted to drugs!" It is no use saying that he began experimenting with drugs in the safe and exclusive environment of the private Quaker school he attended.   Jeremy would not want to hear that; he feels he must put the blame on something outside himself.

After one long session which I can only describe to you 'parent abuse' I said the unsayable and pulled out the trump card, "You had two loving parents even though they made mistakes, you had every   possible opportunity, which is damn sight more than I had when I came to this country alone and with nothing"   The moment those words came out I knew I should not have uttered them, but it was too late, the outburst came out loud and clear " Don't you dare blame me for the war" he said. Please forgive me, Jeremy, I do not blame you. I know that collective suffering is easier to bear, the knowledge that it is not just happening to me is marginally better than the suffering of someone in isolation Let's not get into this one right now. I hope that he knows or that he knew I loved him more than words could say and were it possible I would have sacrificed my own life for him if that meant saving his, because what followed can only be described as the darkest nightmare.

June 1998

Jeremy made a big decision he was ready, he said, to go to a rehabilitation centre and make another fresh start. He admitted to taking large doses of methadone plus vallium and diazepans. Detoxing the body as well as the mind from such heavy dependence was not going to be easy but his mind was made up. Both Michael and I were pleased though naturally anxious, hoping and praying for his success.

Jeremy called a rehab centre himself explaining that he understood his problems very well and asking to be treated like an adult rather than like some young a junkie, teenager. They responded well though there was a big snag. He was told that his daily intake of methadone was much too high, he was on 130mg. daily, and that before being accepted he had 3 weeks to reduce his intake to 80mg. To our still ignorant minds despite the many years of living with an addict, this did not seem to be such an impossible obstacle to overcome but Jeremy expressed doubts about his ability to do this.

I only understand, now when it was too late, that addiction like hunger cannot be explained to those who have not experienced it and who have not lived through it themselves.

We live in a society where we are conditioned to certain responses even those of us who consider ourselves   more   enlightened..   So naturally the conditioned response was 'you can do it if you want it badly enough'. In vain Jeremy tried to explain that methadone was a poison that should never be given as a heroin substitute, that it is long acting and difficult to detox from the body, causing severe pains for many months. He maintained that if he could get pure heroin he would be able to detox with greater ease. Again the alarm bells rang louder,"do you want us to provide you with heroin and become your pushers? Is this what you want?",

"No" he said, "I am only trying to tell you what I think is a better solution to the problem. I will try and do my best but I can't promise.

July 1998

We had not heard from Jeremy for a week since our last conversation. At first I took this to be a good omen; he was trying to sort things out for himself. He told me so many times to let go, not to be anxious just because I do not hear from him for a few days. My anxiety reached a peak when Seamus, his best friend, told me he had left a message on Jeremy's answer-phone to which he had not responded.

I had began rehearsals that week for Herakles, a Greek tragedy by Euripedes. Coming home one evening from rehearsal I went to Jeremy;s flat, banged on the door to no avail. With a dark sense of foreboding I asked his neighbours when they had last seen him. I remember how heavy my body felt walking up the stairs to my home. I did not want to believe it; intuitively I knew. I also saw the fear in Michael's eyes as we discussed asking the police to break in to Jeremy's flat.

I am conscious of these words describing in a simple rather clinical way the course of events that followed that inadequately reflect the pain. Where do we get the strength to overcome the blows that life deals us?

Accompanied by our dearest friend, Seamus, we took a cab to Jeremy's flat. We sat in stony silence sharing the same unexpressed thoughts not wishing to influence each other with the fear we felt in our hearts. As we reached the house where Jeremy lived we saw an ambulance outside in the street and a police car. Now my imagined fear turned into cold stark reality. I rushed up the stairs to be met by a young policewoman asking me to identify myself. I knew then my son was dead. I only begged to be allowed to see him, paradoxically hoping that she would say no! I did not have the strength to face the reality. The police woman seemed kind and supportive she told me that Jeremy had been dead for about 3 or 4 days and that it would be better to remember him the way he was.

The howling and uncensored noise that tore out of my guts practically shook the walls. I could not at that moment share my grief with Michael who I knew was standing by me but whom I hardly saw or even acknowledged. I was alone with my grief and it filled my whole being; the physical pain was tearing me apart. My beautiful son is dead and I will never see him again. I will never argue with him again; talking about argument he won the last one!

He was found with a syringe in his hand. A full bottle of methadone was found in the fridge together with a bottle of vallium pills which seemed to indicate that it was not an act of premeditated suicide otherwise he would have tried to make absolutely sure and take everything at his disposal.

Jeremy had told us that he would do his best, obviously his fear of failure was so great that he tried to do it his way ie. buy the heroin and attempt to substitute it for methadone. We subsequently learned that he was In the process of pawning the most precious thing he had, his drum kit, presumably to buy the heroin. We suspected that whatever he bought was either contaminated with something, always the possibility with street drugs or a pure dose that was simply too strong for him. This knowledge is of little consolation since he is gone and I miss him so much that the pain of it becomes physical. I know that it will never get better. The only thing that is better is the much more diminished fear of my own end.

One thing in the Jewish religion which now makes sense to me is the tradition of sitting 'shiva' for the deceased. Friends and relations coming to sit with the bereaved, talking about the loss, remembering the lost one, crying and laughing as the mood takes them and most important, letting it all out and not holding back or trying to be stoic.

Despite not being in any way religious we were blest with a few such friends who did just that and much more. Our dearest and closest friend, Seamus, an Irish playwright of great intelligence and sensitivity, was both my son's friend as well as Michael's, helped us to live through the hardest time. Jeremy trusted him completely and they both recognised in each other the creative urge, the angst and the pain which is part of human existence. We sat, talked and cried and with Seamus, his wife, Val, Sheila, Michael's sister and my friend Amanda, Sonja and Paul who turned up when we needed them most. How can we ever return such warmth and friendship.

I was deeply hurt and disappointed that none of Michael's relatives got in touch with us after the funeral. I tried to be as rational as I possibly could be under the circumstances. After all we had lived abroad for many years, the family ties had become loose though we had a good or seemingly good rapport with Stephen, Michael's cousin. He knew Jeremy a bit better than other members of the family yet he, too, kept strangely silent. I must tell you that my disappointment turned to bitter anger. There is a kind of emotional constipation which lurks under the skin of the English psyche, the inability to share deep and painful feelings. This view is more charitable than the alternative which is simply that people are indifferent or do not care and I would rather not contemplate that. My cousins in Israel, by the way, proved to be very supportive. They became very close to us in spirit despite the geographic distance and different culture.

Dearest Jeremy I miss you and think of you every hour of my life now and till the very end of time. Life's biggest irony is the fact that we are now in contact with Zac, our beautiful grandson.

L came back from Australia on hearing of Jeremy's death. I always felt that she loved him but could not cope with his addiction; it is difficult to live with the lies, broken promises and up-and-down behaviour. I also thought I perceived her sense of guilt for taking away the most precious thing in his life, his son. In any event I just wanted to embrace her for bringing to us the precious gift that Jeremy left behind. Agony and ecstasy is the only way I can describe our feelings on first seeing Zac on his third birthday. Zac seems not only beautiful but a bright and eloquent little boy with an amazing vocabulary for his age. Both Michael and I tried very hard to curb the flood of emotions for fear of overwhelming him. When he left after the first visit we both howled like injured hyenas knowing how proud Jeremy would have been of his son. It reinforced our loss.

Let me just tell you something that I am aware of every day of my life from now on. I want to live, I want to work I want to see my grandson grow but if I knew that today would be the last day of my life I would accept it I hope with dignity and calm.

I have written a poem for Jeremy but I better tell you now I do not regard myself as a poet. I love and respect poetry and the skill that good poets have of extracting the essence from language and of weaving wonderful images from words. I just write from my gut and here is an example:

For My Dead Son

October 1998.

You are in my heart,

you are in my bones,

you are in my mind,

my thoughts and my gut.

Your presence is constant.

We will never part

and even though I know that you have gone

and your voice is silent and I feel so alone

I know you will be with me

till the end of time.

February 1999

We are seeing quite a lot of our grandson Zac now which is a constant source of joy. I am also trying to develop a relationship with L who I have to acknowledge is a good mother and who I hope will become my daughter-in-law in the strict sense of the word. I will not blame her for the past even though she caused Jeremy so much pain. I will no longer judge her because even though we have not spoken about the past, as yet, I can feel that she knows and understands the journey that she has traveled. At the moment words are not necessary.

This week we were visited by one of my cousins and his wife from Israel and there is something I want to shout from the roof tops. Why is it that when life seems to glide relatively smoothly we care less about others who do not seem to be gliding with us. I have to a large extent neglected my family in Israel and even gave myself excuses for so doing. We left over forty years ago and kept only cursory contact in that time. They are, after all, not a part of my culture, they are Israelis living in their own land. I am a European and quite Anglicised at that; do we have much in common? The answer is, of course, yes. Please do not be embarrassed by my simplistic and sentimental outpouring but when my cousin Edna called me from Israel on hearing of Jeremy's death and saying that both Michael and I have to come to be with them and that the whole family wanted to meet us my heart wanted to burst. My need to be with some members of my family including a whole generation I had not met was overwhelming and my guilt for having distanced myself till now was quite painful.

Miscellaneous Writings to and by my Son.

Dearest Jeremy, for the hundredth time I have been reading some of your writings because it is the only way that I can still talk to you and resuscitate some of our old arguments. Oh what wouldn't I give to have one of those screaming sessions with you when you tried to put the guilt trip on me although I know in your heart of hearts you did not really believe in it. You often accused us of having middle-class values, of wanting to have a lawyer or a doctor for a son. You know this is not true. The moment we discovered your talent for music we did everything to nurture it. You know very well that art for me is the only religion worth believing in and after al, for better or for worse, I am an artist myself and I know something about creative frustration. You know, my darling son, that the only thing not acceptable to us was your drug taking because it was so clear what the drugs were doing not only to your health but your head. I admit that going to New York at the time of your adolescence may not have been a good idea but it never occurred to us to leave you in England. How could we have abandoned you and who was there to leave you with? We were a close-knit family and truly believed that facing up to new challenges and opportunities would be exciting and rewarding. Even now with the tragic hindsight I still do not know what else we could have done.

It is time now to tell you, my reader, that the writings of my son which I am constantly reading and re-reading prove to me that in his schizophrenic state of mind he revealed, at times, unbelievable understanding of his plight and of others, because of drugs, total denial of the situation in which he found himself.

The following are some of the samples for you to judge. I will make no comments on my son's writings suffice it to say that some break my heart and some anger me still and all of them make me cry out for him.

After a particular argument with Michael which was a repetition of all the previous arguments Jeremy wrote:

"You are sick of this and tired of that

And now you want the quiet life

You have done all you can for your troublesome brat

So now you crave the quiet life;

Every man has his limits you say before he seeks the quiet life,

But search and seek it as you may you'll never find

The quiet life

For buried deep in your troubled core the guilt that like a termite gnaws

The feeling that you could not have done more before you sought the quiet life"

The changing moods of my son's condition produced many conflicting thoughts all of them real. the constant fear lurked just under the the skin as expressed in the following verse:

Fear

7/2/97

It's not like you wake up with a start one day

With a huge gaping hole in your soul...nay

It's insidious, starting out small

As a grain of sand.

Then it's the size of a piece of grit

And you wonder why your laughter started to sound so hollow all of a sudden.

Months later slumped on a hospice bed, a friend's bed (if you are lucky enough) your family's bed ditto?

Trying to summon up the facial movements that you think approximate laughter no matter how fucking hollow

And all through the agony the silent despair

The loss of will to fight; they never told you;

HERE LIES....

1961 – 199.....

DIED OF LANCER OF THE SOUL

WHY?

As I copy my sons writings trying so much to keep him alive to make some sense of the agonies he suffered which I know I will never fully understand, all I can hope for is that his words will touch his son when he will be old enough to read them. And maybe he will learn from his father's mistakes and be inspired by his father's talents. Jeremy tried hard to get a council flat and to have his own nest. The only way this was possible to achieve was to declare himself homeless and to move into a hostel to await an allocation. If we had sufficient cash we would have provided him with a flat but the only way this would have been possible would be by selling our flat and buying something in a less desirable part of London. We talked about it a great deal and came to the conclusion that this would have had removed Jeremy's responsibility for coping with his own life and that the pressures bearing upon him may lead him toward making the right decisions and going into treatment. All I can now do is to provide you with his thoughts.

The following was written when Jeremy was living in the hostel.

Room 33

Sept.20th. 1997.

Young kid died in my hostel last night, Room opposite mine

They found him in the morning blue and cold and

down to his last dime,

Traces of tin foil dried up smack running down it,

Broken ampoule on the floor:

His real crime - looking for love, doomed never to have found it.

Most likely his next of kin will scream,

"It was drugs that killed my son"

He will be added to the mountain of statistics

(The evil pushers claimed another one)

Another reason to force through pointless legislation

To keep this cycle of despair in operation,

(after all it's big cbusiness –so many folk like to get high)

And the fat cats mutter "let's put the screws in

tighter cause I want my piece of the pie"

And so I sit here in my room the "warming"

my thawing heart

And I almost feel glad for that lonely young kid has found peace from this madness at last.

I can pass no judgment on my son's state of mind at the time of his writings I just simply wish to share them with you. One thing I know because I have had many arguments with him as to what society should do about the ever increasing drug problem. Jeremy was for the legalization of drugs and although I opposed this for many years I now can see the logic behind such a conviction and I would only add that if we ever came to the conclusion that legalisation was an option it should go together with many, many more treatment centres for which of course adequate funding would be required.

Jeremy's views on the matter were as follows, expressed as a modification of the AA 12 steps:

Alternative 1st.3 steps

Step1

Towards the complete legalization of all drugs and the elimination of our, 'contrived drug problem'

We admitted as a whole that our puritanical, hypocritical, hysterical and blinkered attitude toward those amongst us who wish to partake of substances that have by our own admission been scape-goated falsely blamed and along with those who use them actively persecuted against by our society, has done nothing but genuine harm toward the goal of personal freedom of choice and responsibility to accept any consequences of those choices. That in adopting a falsely superior moral and ethical standpoint we have done nothing but create a so called drug problem, wherein too many people in positions of great power now have a vested interest in keeping the whole cycle of illegality and addiction in full operation since this state of affairs has made the drug trade and pharmaceutical industries one of the largest money spinners the world has ever known.

All at the expense and misery of not only the addict but those people who suffer as a result of desperate and ultimately needless criminal acts, perpetrated by not only the metabolically ill addict, but worst of all the corrupt government officials, doctors judges etc...etc...

Step 2

We came to realise that the majority of the worlds governments have made a massive categorical error in their outlook on the individual's right to take or not to take whatever substances he or she might choose; and that no one has the right to interfere in these most private decisions.

Furthermore the first real step in promoting real individual responsibility is to leave these personal decisions in the hands of the individual and making sure that any interested party have access not only to the substances they want or need but also to have accurate and up-to-date information pertaining to the long and short term effects and side effects of said substances so that their choices are ultimately based on fact rather than scare mongering hysteria and false information springing from a witch-hunt mentality which has until now strangled any progressive ideas in their cradle.

Step 3

Having had the courage to take a long and hard objective view of our drastic failings as a society to deal with these matters and therefore, by implication, just how much personal responsibility the powers that be actually want us to have (after all nothing is more threatening to authority than true autonomy, which again by implication renders authority redundant.)....

We decided collectively that the beginnings of a true and lasting understanding of our self-created problem and one which would direct the way to a basically sane and rational solution to our still ever present need to persecute members of society who we consider to deviate from the norm as it were, would be to take the power to create yet more punitive legislation, which will only perpetuate this cycle of despair, away from the politicians and lobby groups; doctors and so- called 'experts' and once and for all give it to the individual, as was once the case, as recent history will bear out; we have, in order to instigate this process, which is only the beginning in the struggle to understand ourselves - to face our seemingly innate fear of 'chaos' or 'anarchy' - two words that are screamed hysterically whenever the concept of true individual autonomy is raised; finally we must realize collectively our 'fear of freedom' and work toward having the strength to face it and in doing so finally bring about the beginning of real self trust and therefore self rule.

Only then will humankind be ready to grow up and leave our huge kindergarten of bureaucracy and spiritual bankruptcy scape-goating and hysterical scare-mongering.

I have reported Jeremy's thoughts on the subject of drug dependency as I found them. It is interesting to note that there are now disputes and discussions on how best to solve the drug problem and questions are being posed as to the effectiveness of methadone which some doctors now admit is a much harder substance to detox from and in the long run more addictive than pure heroin. In Switzerland successful attempts have been made by distribution of heroin to the addicts under doctor's supervision which cuts out the crime and prevents the drug associated health hazards. But changes of this nature would have to be addressed globally and much more money would have to be spent on treatment clinics. It is also true to say that our attitude to the addicts also would have to change drastically. We still generally view the addict as some one who dropped out of society, the evil-doer lurking around the corner ready to pounce on an innocent bystander and do something atrocious in order to satisfy his or her habit. And of course even though this maybe true there is another class of addicts living under the umbrella of respectability, the doctors, lawyers and the successful entertainers who have enough money to satisfy their cravings and who can afford to get others to do the dirty job for them. I have no desire to be a moralist here, I just wish to tell you that there must be some ways of saving human lives.

It is evident from Jeremy's writings that he desperately wished to rid himself of his addiction, even though he also tried to justify it.

Gathering my son's writing at random I came across many conflicting thoughts and moods that he was going through but one thing remains constant and grows ever more prominent, his sensitivity, his intelligence, his unbearable suffering that no-one could alleviate least of all himself. The following was written by him in March 1998.

"Walking back from the all too familiar battle zone of street drug deals and dodgy deals today I passed the address given to me when I phoned L's house and the new flat mate told me her supposed new address, I couldn't resist walking through the little iron gate to the basement flat and peering inside at the kitchen wall covered in photos.

Although I didn't see anything instantly familiar - the mind can play tricks on you in moments like this and I thought I saw a picture of her - I cast my eye around for any of Zac but there were none. I am sure its not the address but anyhow so what if it is?

Sometimes I look back on this grim decade of the 90's and it strikes me like a blow to the kidneys just how much pain there has been how much loss - sadness - despair-suicidal depression - and sprinkled in between - a little true love and happiness and fulfillment but all as fragile and transient as the wings of a butterfly. I feel as though I have seen far too much sorrow for my years and at times the sheer weight of it seems to make me physically exhausted. It's such a paradox, I know I have the capacity to give so much to love life on it's own terms as it were - and yet nearing 37 years I feel like an old man inside, an old man who has lost everything precious to him - living out his remaining days with his whole consciousness and being on auto pilot plus his emotional denial and armour as thick as a bank vault to stop himself from just dropping dead of a broken heart and spirit.

Although I may never see my son again I pray constantly for his well-being and happiness and I hope that perhaps one day we will reunite in a real bond of father and son. I am so alone inside so desolate that it transcends any notion of self pity or some such ridiculous phrase - sometimes it seems almost to take on a religious quality especially since it's so intertwined with the hopeless sadness and struggles of the human condition as a whole.

God grant me the serenity

To accept the things I cannot change

Courage to change the things I can

And the wisdom to know the difference

(and all that god shit)

Amen

I found in Jeremy's writings a collection of poems that obviously spoke to him and which he understood not only intellectually but viscerally and appear to reflect his feelings. I want you to know these poems:

ALCHEMY OF SUFFERING

by C Baudelaire

Nature glows with this man's joy,

Dims with another's grief;

What signifies the grave to one

is glory to the next,

Trismegistus intercedes:

This ever daunting guide

makes me a midas in reverse,

Saddest of Alchemists

Gold turns to iron at my touch,

Heaven darkens to hell;

Clouds become a winding-sheet

To shroud my cherished dead,

And on celestial shores I build

Enormous sepulchres.

****

THE FOUNTAIN OF BLOOD

Sometimes I feel my blood is spilling out

In sobs, the way a fountain overflows

I know I hear it, sighing as it goes,

And search my flesh but cannot find the wound;

It turns the stones to archipelagoes,

As if the city were a battleground,

Slaking the thirst of every living thing

And dyeing all the world of nature red.

How often have I called for wine to drug

If only foe a day, this wasting fear-

My ears grow sharp on wine, my eyes grow clear!

In love I have sought an hour 's oblivion-

But love to me is a pallet stuffed with pins

That drains away my blood for whores to drink!

****

I am not searching out examples to portray my son's high taste in literature nor am I interested in presenting his literary talent for you to appreciate. I just turn the half torn pages of his writings, they were not even diaries and in them I look closer into his tormented soul.

Since his death I am finally getting to know him in a way I did not know him in life.

Here is something he must have written after a visit to the dole office.

CASE WORKER

You give yourself away It's in your eyes

They radiate as much compassion for the

Suffering of rejects of society, the oppressed and desperate

As two puddles of urine.

You relish your small allowance of power jealously

Guarding it like any good control freak;

Doling out your good news with an almost reluctant air

Whilst relishing the times when you can really screw some poor helpless wretch;

I can see you in my mind's eye almost gibberish with delight as you ooze out the words "I'm sorry

we can't help you at all goodbye"

Jeremy and I often talked and sometimes argued about the position of a 'victim' in our society. Is it possible to pull yourself by the bootstraps from any environment which a chance of birth has placed one? Obviously there are people who try and 'drown' there are people who give up the fight and there are those who persevere against all odds.

Since I have tended to see Jeremy's problem as self-imposed, I sometimes took the tough line of "You did it to yourself and only you can do something about it" I do not know now in retrospect if this was entirely true and I do feel tormented by guilt which I must not allow to swallow me up. Living with an addict is not an easy matter as anyone with similar experience will attest but Jeremy as I have pointed out was an extremely sensitive individual and there is a theory although not scientifically proven that children of Holocaust survivors bear a heavy guilt for the parent's experiences which they find hard to come to terms with.

I find it very hard to copy the next bit of writing that Jeremy wrote to his father who loved him so much but who found dealing with his addiction problem even harder than I.

EXPECTATIONS

"I come to you for....Comfort?

I come to you as son to father

My soul burning with mortal pain

I come to you...to hear from your lips, your own lips

That I am OK?

I come to you for communication, spirit to spirit;

soul to soul.

I am told that perhaps I must accept that I will never

find what I seek;

That I am looking for what isn't there;

And that is the end...every man is alone;

And yes! every man is alone:

So excuse me for suffering under the delusion that family means something!

That perhaps, just perhaps it could be an oasis in

our aloneness.

Do excuse me...it will never happen again.

But I came to you because you helped to bring me into...this place

I didn,'t ask for it did I?

And in coming to you, father, well...

That's nature in action isn't it?

I will add something here not to soften the blow because I want you to know everything and in my pain I no longer care if I come out as a 'reasonable person' but I want you to know that both of us said one thing often "We love you Jeremy more than we can say and we will do anything to help but we do not love the addict in you"

I know that at some deep unconscious level Jeremy knew and understood that as some of his other writings indicate.

27/5/98

Two days after my 37th birthday I have been thinking back through all that has happened in the last 7 years since I turned 30.

The number 7 being the magical number that it is.

There is no question that I have once again it seems come full circle and am now at the bottom of the pit that I started the long and arduous journey climbing out of at the age of 26. I suppose I just have to keep telling myself that I am still a warrior! I still have the fight in me, because if not I may as well resign myself to a life of dependency on drugs which deep down I know I don't want for the simple reason that if I did want it I would not feel so much of a failure....nor feel so much pain over the issue...I would have resigned myself to it long time ago (and at least that in itself would have brought me some semblance of peace of mind.)

But once again I stand at a crossroad and the path I choose - when I start down it, instead of just standing here stationary - will determine my fate and my destiny...and perhaps as the rune stones that I cast a few days ago said ; it is time to take that giant leap of faith into the unknown....just surrendering with total trust to the healing power, both inside and outside of me.

MAJOR PROBLEM?

I do not subscribe to the method of treatment known as the 12 step programme. When you are clean and attending meetings it is of course easy to take what you need from a meeting and leave what you don't need behind. In primary treatment it is a different story altogether, you either surrender your will completely.....or you are considered 'not serious about getting well' ....I do not subscribe to 12 step belief system or even the fact that addiction according to them is a disease. It is after all only a belief system and having been through it quite a few times before I know that it is completely impossible for me to accept. But that by no means suggests that I do not want to stop my dependency on drugs. And the two attitudes are not incompatible - as long as I am in an environment that understands this!

DETOX. This must be flexible and I must be treated as an adult who knows what he needs instead of some lying Junkie who only wants to get as many drugs as possible and therefore my attitudes are ignored.

I have experienced this and it is absolutely scandalous that addicts who wish to stop their addictions are treated in this way!

It is obvious from the above how much my son struggled with the plight he was in. The inner thoughts and outward arguments were so different. I understand now only too late and too well that his fear of failure was so great and that no matter how much he wanted to be clean he also wanted our acceptance of him as he was and that is the only thing we could not give him,Ä¶and maybe and I repeat maybe we should have done? On May14th 1998 Jeremy wrote the following:

As the inevitable 'final' confrontation looms near the last fight for my life, and any chance I may still have of finally really changing gear in my life and paving the way for the best chance I have of peace of mind, of being at peace with myself, at least on some level and fighting tooth and nail for the last chance to fulfill my true potential; I feel, at least at the moment that a strange almost dreamlike calm has taken possession of me, it is a calm born out of the knowledge that I can really do it this time, or is it the natural denial that overtakes people when faced with a massive and terrifying decision or task which they know there is no turning away from; unless for good - and that equals-death. I do not feel scared by the, 'sacrifice' of 'abstinence' for however long that may go on....I am of course terrified of failing and of the consequent turning of backs that would go with it; the backs of my parents, what few friends I have and lastly the turning of my own back on myself.

As the runes said 'massive leap of faith is required -jumping empty handed into a void. And the hard work I have to face I must undertake to do joyously. I am a survivor and surviving this in itself will renew my inner and outer strength to a degree I never thought possible.

The following was found undated.

I must get the fuck out of here! of this situation. I must as Charlie pointed out yesterday undergo a complete revolution of the mind body soul and spirit if I am to get through this living death of a life because if not one thing is certain it won‚Äôt be a living death any longer.   I will fast check out of here over and out....and what a tragic waste of someone who has as much to offer as I do because I know I do. What I don't know is whether or not I can actually do it - actually detox from the huge amount of drugs I am on. That thought scares the shit out of me, since if I knew beyond the shadow of a doubt that I could'nt I really would end this living hell once and for all.

Thank God that there are some things better left unanswered and unknown. I would give one of my eyes to be clean again....I would give all I possess for I know that once I am clean the energy to replace whatever I may have lost would be therein abundance!

I know this is my last chance and I must grab it. Being off drugs combined with what I know now what I have learned I would become a very strong individual indeed.

God grant me the serenity

To accept the things I cannot change

Courage to change the things I can

And the wisdom to know the difference.

Amen

This above paragraph is like a 'prayer' said at the end of every 12 step programme meeting.

As I continue to find my son's writings of his feelings and thoughts I want to include them immediately disregarding the time sequence in which they were written like his changing moods, constantly alternating between trying to justify his drug taking, sometimes trying to blame outside forces for his actions, sometimes expressing such unbelievable desire to get off the drug taking 'merry-go- round' and to become healthy and clean. One thing which remains constant is his utter honesty with himself, his ability to be in touch with his innermost feelings even if those feelings fluctuated from time to time.

Jeremy's frustrations with himself have often manifested themselves in his physical behaviour. One day after having an argument with his musician friend he banged the front door with his fist. I wrote the following:

Everytime I open my front door

I look at the thin round ridge just below the key hole

The indentation of your fist that shuttered the wood

The rage you must have felt

When you punched in the door now repaired

And smoothed out except for that thin ridge

I am so glad it is still there

I slide my fingers over that ridge and kiss the cold

wood

Calming my own rage because you are not there.

I really do not care anymore whether I appear self indulgent and bathe in my sorrow and plead with you to understand the pain that I know for sure will never go away. In some ways it is worse now because I cannot talk about it any longer and burden my friends with facts they already know. And I now know for sure that you can only talk to people who have lost their sons or daughters in similar circumstances, they will understand but I do not know many not personally anyway.

In April 1996 Jeremy wrote the following:

In Greek mythology there was a man named Sisyphus who because of some serious transgression against one God or Goddess was condemned for all eternity to push a huge bolder up a hill and just when he reached the top his strength gave out or he would slip and the boulder would go crushing and tumbling down to the bottom of the hill.

Sisyphus would have to start all over again pushing this huge round rock up the hill and again just as he got to the top it would go crashing down to the bottom again, ...ad infinitum.

This little glimpse into one man's eternal hell could be a metaphor for many things; it seems to me at this moment in time to be a metaphor, or even a summing up of my life's achievement so far, the only difference perhaps being that on occasions I have been allowed some rest from this torture either at the bottom of the hill or at the top, where perhaps I have grown cocky and complacent and sitting to admire the view thinking I've made it at last. I have failed to notice how precariously the boulder is resting and with a start of terror looking round to see the rock plummeting down to the bottom again. Because you see to explain what to me obviously doesn't need explanation; the boulder is all my hopes and dreams and plans, values, aspirations, loves and fascinations, my wants my needs, my talents....The hill is life or my life as I repeat the same mistakes, trying so desperately to learn from them sometimes thinking or really feeling deep down that I have succeeded; other times knowing that I have failed to grasp the lesson and the freedom it brings (or rather the freedom inherent in really learning your lesson your truth).

But right now in my shattered life it seems that the rock is getting heavier; and the hill steeper and all I really want to do is to let go the rock send it hurtling into the void or somewhere else where it might be caught by a pair of hands to whom it does not seem so heavy! And to see the ever steepening hill suddenly even out into a beautiful gentle slope easier to walk along.

Or maybe, just maybe I can finally place the boulder firmly and securely in its resting place atop this hill, for it is really a thing of beauty and should be seen by others, a monument to the fact that you really can after all the sadness, desperation anger loss of hope, rigour and vitality start over all over and make your life work for you.

It is my one and only hope .....I want to love life again!

There is not much I can say after that. Yes I do blame myself for not discussing with Jeremy, his thoughts, his feelings after he let me read the above. I did try but by that time his cynicism was a great barrier and his suspicion of any psychiatric help suggested on several occasions totally overwhelming, he was always a step ahead of any questions or suggestions which might be posed by a counsellor saying that he knew himself better than anyone else and that he asked himself all the questions and tormented himself by the answers.

You will probably wish to know how I cope? How does any mother cope with the greatest loss that can befall on anyone, the death of one's child before one's own death. It does not seem natural but then when I start thinking about it, the tragic life of my aunt Lola rushes into my head. As I already told you she had two beautiful and healthy children, a girl of 5 and a boy of 7, shot by the Nazis for no reason, no reason at all, cutting short their young lives before they even began. I ask myself what gave her the strength to survive this tragedy. Maybe there is no comparison, the suffering we have to go through in our lives is not measured by some 'suffering' thermometer, telling us this degree of suffering is greater or more acceptable than another degree; you cannot measure pain in such a way. My aunt died with a picture of her children in her arms. The only thing one can say about it is that experiencing the loss one can understand others without resorting to words.

Jeremy suffered because he was so caught in the web from which he could not perceive of any possible escape, blaming himself, blaming us blaming the society in which he lived wanting desperately to change but being so terrified of failure. I understand it so well now and I do feel guilty for not easing his pain although I ask myself constantly "how could I have done so?"

Jeremy wrote a most beautiful poem which was set to music by a wonderful singer, Helen Chadwick, who tells me that every time she sings the poem it touches so many people:

Testament

If I could play, on a drum…

A rhythm

That would heal (wounded souls)

That would strengthen (weakened bodies)

That would soothe (tortured spirits….

If I could capture, in a melody,

The sweet sad music of humanity;

Struggling in the dark....

To find meaning for all the madness, murder,

Mayhem....

And if I could write a testament of words

That would, perhaps just come close

To expressing my love...

For you,

For all you mean to me

So you would really know it's strength

Then all of this will not have been in vain.

And one thing more...

I would play that drum

And sing that melody

And write those sacred words....

For everyone

Again...and again...and again.....

At the bottom of this poem Jeremy wrote; (Now I know I am ripe for the loony bin)

As though having such deep feeling and expressing them is the right of the madman. But here too is a poem which he chose and carefully copied written by *C Baudelaire*

THE PIPE

I am a writer's pipe. One look at me,

And the coffee colour of my Kaffir face

Will tell you I am not the only slave:

My master is addicted to his vice.

Every so often he is overcome

By some despair or other, whereupon

Tobacco clouds pour out of me as if

The stove were kindled and the pot put on.

I wrap his soul in mine and cradle it

within a blue and fluctuating thread

that rises out of my rekindled lips

From the glowing coal that brews a secret spell,

He smokes his pipe, allaying heart and mind,

And for tonight all injuries are healed.

Needless to say Jeremy's choice of poetry was the reflection of his being. I hope that he derived some solace from it because he knew that he wasn't alone. I would like to give you a small example of Jeremy's lighter side and his sometimes delicious sense of humour.

When Michael retired from his job at UNICEF he studied Shiatsu, a form of acupressure, without the use of needles. He practised on a number of our friends and on me as well as Jeremy.

I found the following which he wrote for his Dad one day:

There was a man from Belsize Park

Who practised Shiatsu after dark

People came who felt uptight

And he'd press points that would put them right

He'd stretch and squeeze and twist and turn

Do everything except a Chinese burn

Many grunts and groans came from his den

And all in the name of good old Zen

Many a poor soul would think as they knocked at his door

Which pain is worse after or before?

So next time you have a nagging back ache

Sit down take an aspirin and wait!!!!

It is my son's humour that I miss so much, despite the pain, the agony and the nearly always present anxiety we had such good times and so many laughs.

I wrote the following for Jeremy when the sadness of missing him had to find some outlet.

Now that you have gone,

I no longer cling to life, with a force and desire

Which was a part of my being,

Like a well worn out piece of elastic

I still hold on to life

But the hold is so much looser and if one day it snaps

I will let it go, there is nothing I fear more

than loneliness or meaningless existence

And even though your seed is here in the form of a beautiful boy

He is only a quarter mine

And you who were so much of me

Will not be here to hold my hand

When I shall need it the most.

Sometimes little objects spark off an image and I have to write it down. The following is an example of such feelings:

Every day I look at the Macondi sculpture you gave me one Xmas. It's shape tall and very thin reminds me of you. The body caved in, knees slightly bent. Your body so beautiful and strong looked like the sculpture when you are 'using'. When the drugs seemed to shrink you and you looked like you were about to topple over, my beautiful son so shrunken and weary of life. I said to you "you will never live to see your 40th birthday unless you make an enormous effort to do something positive about your condition".

I didn't understand till now that you were beyond that act of will Please forgive me!

Jeremy died of an overdose on the 27th June 1998

I can think of no better epitaph for you, Jeremy, than this quotation from RM Rilke

Sonnets to Orpheus

Set up no stone for his memory,

Just let the rose bloom each year

For his sake......

And as for you, my friend. my story is drawing to an end, I keep up such a good pretense. What helps me enormously is the fact that I am a performer and when I get work I put all my energies into my work. I had two plays written for me by the writer and director, Julia Pascal, with whom I have worked for the last 10 years and hope to continue to do so. Julia helped me enormously, not only in my acting career but also in opening many 'emotional' doors t hat had been firmly shut for a long time.

I am conscious of having a public face and a private one. In private I live with my loss, I talk to Jeremy, I think about him every day of my life, I think about the irony of losing a son and gaining a grandson since had Jeremy lived I doubt very much that I would have been able to see Zac unless Jeremy and L's relationship would miraculously have improved and if, of course, and this is the big 'IF' Jeremy would become completely 'clean'. But life is so full of IF'S.

The reality of life is the fact that people and those one calls friends cannot give one the understanding and the continuous support one craves and life has to return to a 'normal' rhythm. I am lucky I suppose in that I have a loving and supportive husband although I also know that he deals with his pain differently, more inwardly and I have to respect that. Both of us are striving to establish a better relationship with L, we respect her desire for independence and hope that she will also feel at home with us.

I am also so far blessed with inordinate amount of energy maybe due to the fact that I was once a dancer and am still capable at the age of nearly 70 to have a job which demands physical stamina and expression.

I play the role of Mother-earth at the Millennium Dome and I stand up there 30 meters up above the ground watching the crowd, and thinking "yes I am still here". I often think of the wonderful quotation from Shakespeare's 'As You Like It'

All the world's a stage

And all the men and women merely players:

And one man in his time

plays many parts

His acts being seven ages.....

July the 18th, 1999

We are going to Brighton to visit Jeremy's grave or to be more precise the place where his ashes buried. L and Zac are coming with us. I hope L can make peace with Jeremy and I hope I will be able to look upon all of us with some grace. In the meantime I want to let you read the simple poem I wrote for Jeremy on the anniversary of his death.

It is a year now since you left this world, Maybe with relief, for your life was so full of sadness.

But I only remember you as my beautiful blue- eyed boy

With long cascading hair and a face of an angel.

I miss you just as much now as I did when you left us, I hold on to you so very very tight

You are with me

Every day and every step of my life!

How does one cope with grief and especially the loss of one's child. The grief does not go away nor diminish with the passage of time. On the contrary it gets worse. Because I do not talk about him as much I miss him more and it is very painful. I need to work and be busy and focus on other things. I cannot expect my friends to be sorry for me and offer me perpetual support and comfort. In fact we lost our dear friend, Seamus, due to difference of opinion on certain political issues something which I find very difficult to come to terms with. To my mind no political issue is worth the price of friendship but this alas is not a view held by everyone.

I resist feeling sorry for myself. I feel more sorry for the wonderful human being that was my son and the great things he had to offer but as I wrote in the last poem he is with me every day of my life! I am proud to have given birth to him and to have had him for 37 years of his life with all the joy and the pain and the anxiety and the frustrations that living with him entailed.

London 2002

Epilogue

Many years ago I taught at the Julliard School in New York in the drama department and I recollect a very special event:

The great playwright, Arthur Miller came to talk to the students about his work and answer questions. One of the questions stuck in my mind all these years.

"Why is it" asked one of the students "you always write about families. it seems to be the major topic in all your plays?"

The great man thought for a brief second and replied " family is the microcosm of society and I know not of any other institution where people can push each other to the brink of despair or where love and sacrifice can be manifested as much as destruction. So you see it is a big and rich palate to draw from".

I often think it would have been better to experience the depth of some of the emotions than be deprived and never to have had them at all.

All my family with the exception of one who died of natural causes has been killed by the Nazis in the 2nd world war

All my life I have been yearning for the unconditional love which one can only find in a normal family. Having had one son who tragically died of drug overdose left me completely bereft increasing the sense of emptiness. I am lucky and blessed with a good marriage so why am I so greedy?

I remember clearly talking about families when I was young and thinking so long as one has some good friends families are not important we cannot choose our families but we can choose our friends.

So is this persistent feeling of deprivation something which creeps up on one in old age? I wonder?

My grandson who I hope will be fortunate enough to have his own family cannot be burdened with my needs and expectations at the moment if ever.

It is unfortunate that I have not been able to establish closer ties with his mother and her relatives maybe there are too many stumbling blocks too many closed doors which will probably remain shut for ever.

2012

Printed in Great Britain
by Amazon